Palgrave Studies in Educational Futures

Series Editor
jan jagodzinski
Department of Secondary Education
University of Alberta
Edmonton, AB, Canada

The series Educational Futures would be a call on all aspects of education, not only specific subject specialist, but policy makers, religious education leaders, curriculum theorists, and those involved in shaping the educational imagination through its foundations and both psychoanalytical and psychological investments with youth to address this extraordinary precarity and anxiety that is continually rising as things do not get better but worsen. A global de-territorialization is taking place, and new voices and visions need to be seen and heard. The series would address the following questions and concerns. The three key signifiers of the book series title address this state of risk and emergency:

1. **The Anthropocene**: The 'human world,' the world-for-us is drifting toward a global situation where human extinction is not out of the question due to economic industrialization and overdevelopment, as well as the exponential growth of global population. How to we address this ecologically and educationally to still make a difference?
2. **Ecology**: What might be ways of re-thinking our relationships with the non-human forms of existence and in-human forms of artificial intelligence that have emerged? Are there possibilities to rework the ecological imagination educationally from its over-romanticized view of Nature, as many have argued: Nature and culture are no longer tenable separate signifiers. Can teachers and professors address the ideas that surround differentiated subjectivity where agency is no long attributed to the 'human' alone?
3. **Aesthetic Imaginaries**: What are the creative responses that can fabulate aesthetic imaginaries that are viable in specific contexts where the emergent ideas, which are able to gather heterogeneous elements together to present projects that address the two former descriptors: the Anthropocene and the every changing modulating ecologies. Can educators drawn on these aesthetic imaginaries to offer exploratory hope for what is a changing globe that is in constant crisis?

The series Educational Futures: Anthropocene, Ecology, and Aesthetic Imaginaries attempts to secure manuscripts that are aware of the precarity that reverberates throughout all life, and attempts to explore and experiment to develop an educational imagination which, at the very least, makes conscious what is a dire situation.

More information about this series at
http://www.palgrave.com/gp/series/15418

Cathryn van Kessel

An Education in 'Evil'

Implications for Curriculum,
Pedagogy, and Beyond

Cathryn van Kessel
University of Alberta
Edmonton, AB, Canada

Palgrave Studies in Educational Futures
ISBN 978-3-030-16604-5   ISBN 978-3-030-16605-2   (eBook)
https://doi.org/10.1007/978-3-030-16605-2

Library of Congress Control Number: 2019936147

© The Editor(s) (if applicable) and The Author(s), under exclusive license to Springer
Nature Switzerland AG 2019
This work is subject to copyright. All rights are solely and exclusively licensed by the
Publisher, whether the whole or part of the material is concerned, specifically the rights
of translation, reprinting, reuse of illustrations, recitation, broadcasting, reproduction
on microfilms or in any other physical way, and transmission or information storage and
retrieval, electronic adaptation, computer software, or by similar or dissimilar methodology
now known or hereafter developed.
The use of general descriptive names, registered names, trademarks, service marks, etc. in this
publication does not imply, even in the absence of a specific statement, that such names are
exempt from the relevant protective laws and regulations and therefore free for general use.
The publisher, the authors and the editors are safe to assume that the advice and
information in this book are believed to be true and accurate at the date of publication.
Neither the publisher nor the authors or the editors give a warranty, express or implied,
with respect to the material contained herein or for any errors or omissions that may have
been made. The publisher remains neutral with regard to jurisdictional claims in published
maps and institutional affiliations.

Cover illustration: © Mihai Popa/Stockimo/Alamy Stock Photo

This Palgrave Macmillan imprint is published by the registered company Springer Nature
Switzerland AG
The registered company address is: Gewerbestrasse 11, 6330 Cham, Switzerland

PREFACE

I was teaching a Grade 11 Social Studies class in Alberta in the 2008/2009 academic year. It was my first time teaching the course, and I was determined to do the curriculum justice, particularly the history of the Second World War. The theme of the course was nationalism, and I was teaching a set of lessons on genocide within the unit on ultranationalism. I knew that I wanted my students to go beyond the dehumanizing task of memorizing death tolls, and I thought that I had the solution—I would show them original video footage from Auschwitz.

The bell rang to begin class, and I had the video cued up and ready to go. The students settled into their seats, and I quickly explained that, further to our discussions of the Holocaust/Shoah from the last class (which admittedly were more so lists of names, dates, and contexts than "discussions"), we were going to watch a video that showed us more. The video barely finished when the bell that indicated the end of class rang. I turned on the lights to see many students in tears, and those who were not crying nonetheless looked like they had been punched in the stomach. I did not prepare them for that experience, nor did I debrief them. I watched them as they descended into despair and anger regarding the horrors they just encountered. I wish I had known this at the time, but Roger Simon (2014) aptly identified this problem in the context of exhibitions as "undirected emotions" (p. 194).

Luckily, at least some of those students could rise above my naïve, terrible pedagogy and became determined to prevent contemporary genocides—one even worked to raise awareness about the genocide in Darfur

vi   PREFACE

that was raging at the time. I was left with a question festering in my mind and body—How might I engage with historical and contemporary tragedies in a respectful way, neither reproducing emotional pornography nor limiting discussions to cliché or surface-level information? This question eventually led me to pursue doctoral work at the University of Alberta.

Although I began with a specific question about how I might teach about genocide with high school students, it did not take long for my inquiry to expand into the topic of evil. I began by having my mind opened by Alain Badiou's (1993/2001) understandings of evil as betrayal, simulacrum, and disaster. I came to understand that seeing evil as a *process* instead of a *thing* had enormous potential for how we might understand the past as well as give ourselves the tools to make changes needed for societies to hurt less. Not long into my Ph.D. I presented at a conference, where an audience member from my presentation—a scholar from Germany—mentioned that I might be interested in the work of Hannah Arendt (1963/2006), particularly the banality of evil, that describes how some people contribute to violence and atrocities without intending to do so. Here is where my philosophical travels began. I saw the value in both Arendt and Badiou's theories, each proposing a helpful way to think about the ugliness of humans and human societies as at least partly in the domain of ordinary, average people. Soon thereafter, my dalliances with a few other philosophers also turned into longer-term investigations. Adding Ernest Becker to my theoretical toolkit complemented Arendt—while she explained how someone like you or me could perpetuate great harm without intending to, Becker (1975) explained how an ordinary person could delight in causing harm when they saw themselves as a hero fighting evil. In a horrible irony, we create evil by trying to conquer it. I also became interested in very radical ways of understanding evil, such as Jean Baudrillard's (1990/1993, 2004/2005) idea of *Symbolic Evil*. Admittedly, I hated Baudrillard when I first read him, but I am grateful that I continued reading. With each understanding of evil, I felt that there was an opportunity to think and rethink how and why terrible things happen, thus opening up new possibilities for curriculum and pedagogy.

My seemingly odd passion for evil eventually became a course at the university for senior undergraduate and graduate students. We met over several Saturdays, each day discussing a different conceptualization of evil and working together to consider how we might relate those ideas to our own work as teachers, researchers, school leaders, and community members. It is from those classes that I derive this book. It is my hope that each chapter can stand alone, but be more powerful in combination. Perhaps readers might undertake a similar journey to my own—realizing that there are so many ways to springboard discussions about how we might live together on this planet.

Edmonton, Canada   Cathryn van Kessel

REFERENCES

Arendt, H. (2006). *Eichmann in Jerusalem: A report on the banality of evil.* New York, NY: Penguin. (Original work published in 1963)

Badiou, A. (2001). *Ethics: An essay on the understanding of evil* (P. Hallward, Trans.). London, UK: Verso. (Original work published in 1993)

Baudrillard, J. (1993). *The transparency of evil* (J. Benedict, Trans.). London, UK: Verso. (Original work published in 1990)

Baudrillard, J. (2005). *The intelligence of evil or the lucidity pact* (C. Turner, Trans.). Oxford, UK: Berg. (Original work published in 2004)

Becker, E. (1975). *Escape from evil.* New York, NY: Free Press.

Simon, R. (2014). *A pedagogy of witnessing: Curatorial practice and the pursuit of social justice.* Albany, NY: SUNY Press.

Acknowledgements

Writing this book has felt like a rite of passage between my doctoral studies and my work as an early-career academic. I have been lucky to have had the support of colleagues, friends, and family during this process. I am deeply grateful for their insights (and pep talks).

My heartfelt thanks to my father, Hans van Kessel, as well as my friends and graduate students who read chapters (some multiple times!) and offered feedback: Kara Boucher, Francesca Catena, Garret Lashmar, Nick Jacobs, and Andy Scott. They helped me to develop my ideas, and, importantly, make those ideas accessible to my future readers. I could not have done this project without them!

Many thanks to my mentors, Kent den Heyer and jan jagodzinski. Kent guided me as my doctoral supervisor and helped me through the process of rigorous thinking. He seemed to always know when I needed help and when I needed to sort things out on my own. I strive to be a similar mentor to my own graduate students. Without the encouragement of jan, I would not have written this book. His faith in me has seemed unwavering, and he helped guide me through the process of conceptualizing a book and approaching a publisher.

I would also like to thank those who have written articles with me on subjects related to this book. I am indebted to the following people: Kevin Burke, Ryan Crowley, Kent den Heyer, Kip Kline, Rebeka Plots, and my husband, Jeff Schimel. They not only contributed their scholarly insights, but also helped me figure out my own thinking. I have learned, and continue to learn, so much from them.

x   ACKNOWLEDGEMENTS

I could not have survived the creation of this book or even the process of completing my Ph.D. without the help of women I admire and respect. Special thanks to Erin Adams, Adriana Boffa, Kara Boucher, Neelam and Saliha Chattoo, as well as my mother, Anne, and my sister, Janna, for always believing in me.

Last, but certainly not least, I would like to thank my husband, Jeff, and son, Jack, for their support. Mere "thanks" is insufficient for the love and support they have shown me, and for the inspiration, they spark every day.

CONTENTS

1	**Introduction**	1
	Difficult Knowledge and Radical Hope	1
	On Defining Evil	2
	Evil in Educational Research	4
	Using the Label of Evil	5
	Evil and Historical Trauma	7
	Censorship and Ideological Schooling	9
	The State of Educational Research on Evil	12
	Structure of the Book	12
	References	14
2	**Evil Is in the Eye of the Beholder**	19
	Evil as a Category	19
	Immanuel Kant's Radical Evil	21
	The Importance of Intent and Conscious Choices	22
	A Priori Evil vs. a Priori Good	23
	The Evil of Wétiko	24
	A Spectrum of Evil in Popular Film and Television	26
	Empathetic Evil	26
	Anti-Heroes	30
	Domesticated Evils	31
	A Range of Evil	33
	References	33

3 Banal Evil and Social Studies Education   37

Hannah Arendt   37
Radical Evil   38
The Banality of Good and Evil   39
   Ordinary People and Evil   39
   The Wrong Man for a Good Theory   41
Intensive and Extensive Evil   42
Villainification   43
   Meaningful Complexity   45
   The Banality of Evil and Villainification   45
Anti-villainification in Practice   46
   Specific Examples of Banal Evil   47
   Troubling the Singular Agency of Supervillains   48
   Ethical Entanglements   50
   Attention to Language and Phrasing   52
   Teaching Disobedience   54
Implications of Anti-villainification   55
References   57

4 Processes of Evil as a Supplement to Citizenship Education   63

Alain Badiou   63
Contexts for Citizenship Education   64
Badiou's General Anthropology of Truths   65
   Truth Procedures   68
   Fidelity to Our Truth Procedures   70
The Three Evils   70
   Betrayal   71
   Simulacrum   71
   Disaster   73
Eventful Education   73
   Education by the State vs. by Truths   74
   Politics of Difference and Democratic Education   75
   Education as Affirmative Invention   76
Evil Education as Love for the World?   76
References   79

5	**The Politics of Evil**	83
	The Power of Evil	83
	Phenomenography of Evil	85
	Demographic Information	87
	Analysis	87
	Student Understandings of Evil	88
	Evil as Images	89
	Evil as Affects (Bodily) and Effects (Cognitive)	91
	Evil as Distinctly Human (Mostly)	92
	Evil as Subjective	94
	Evil as Abnormal, Extraordinary	96
	Politics of Evil	99
	Conclusions	102
	References	103
6	***Symbolic Evil* and the Schooling System**	107
	Jean Baudrillard	107
	Symbolic Evil	108
	(Mis)Managing Evil	109
	The Accursed Share	110
	Stockpiling the Past	112
	Attempts to Control the Unpleasant	113
	Creative Energy	114
	An Education System for Evil	115
	Student "Success"	116
	Corporations, Jobs, and Schooling	117
	Classroom Climate	119
	Fatal Strategies	120
	References	121
7	**Evil, Existential Terror, and Classroom Climate**	125
	Ernest Becker	125
	Frightened to Death	126
	Terror Management Theory	128
	Teaching as an Immortality Project	130
	Resistances to Divergent Viewpoints	134
	Worldview Threat	135

xiv CONTENTS

Defensive Reactions and Mortality Salience	137
Discounting Other Views in a Classroom	138
Two Concluding Quotations	139
References	140

8 Epilogue 145
References 148

Index 151

CHAPTER 1

Introduction

This is a book about evil in the context of education and how we might live together on this planet in less harmful ways. Evil might seem like a strange choice to explore options for better relations with each other (and certainly I am often the object of odd looks at academic conferences), but I feel that this area of inquiry can help those interested in education think through ethical issues in curriculum, pedagogy, and perhaps even in their daily lives. In his poem, *In Tenebris II*, Thomas Hardy declared how in a future yet to come (when things are supposedly good), society will not tolerate the person "Who holds that if a way to the better there be, it exacts a full look at the Worst." Even in our present times, though, investigating the Worst is not a popular stance or perhaps is fetishized in a sort of masochistic context. In this book, I hope to avoid both foibles, neither ignoring evil nor glorifying it.

Difficult Knowledge and Radical Hope

The evils of historical and contemporary times can be what Deborah Britzman (1998) has called *difficult knowledge*. We might mourn events like war, slavery, genocide, famine, bigotry, and other injustices that reveal suffering to be caused by human indifference or disdain. We can also see difficult knowledge as the range of challenging emotions related to the uncertainty we can feel as we strive for more harmonious relations:

© The Author(s) 2019
C. van Kessel, *An Education in 'Evil'*,
Palgrave Studies in Educational Futures,
https://doi.org/10.1007/978-3-030-16605-2_1

wishing to approach new experiences and new knowledge, feeling both the fatigue of limit and the excitement of potential, and then solving this ambivalence by seeking continuity with the safety of the old objects yet still agitated by the crisis of dependency. (Britzman, 2013, p. 101)

This task, then, is a sort of "radical hope" in the sense of Jonathan Lear (2006)—not being glibly optimistic, but instead tapping into our shared vulnerability. For this shared sense of precarity, we need to see others as mutually alive, and thus, their suffering and deaths as equally able to be grieved (Butler, 2004, 2009). Yet, we do not value each other as such: "precariousness is a universal of human life, yet we experience it in highly singular ways" (Ruti, 2017, p. 94). Not only recognizing our own experiences with precarity might be difficult knowledge, but also recognizing our part in systems that create precarious situations for others—indeed, both are realizations we might rather avoid. Lisa Farley (2009) has aptly noted that Lear highlighted "a possibility that we might prefer to forget: namely, that what matters to us most—our ways of doing things in the world—are at constant risk of coming undone, and becoming our undoing" (p. 546). Indeed, how might we live with the difficult knowledge that surrounds us and our existence in societies?

The theme of this book is that although it may be uncomfortable to discuss evil, it is nonetheless important. Everyone has a sense of what evil is, but many of us ponder neither its nature nor how it functions, let alone how someone's understanding can be different from another person's, or even how the same person might hold multiple conceptualizations over time or even simultaneously. It is no easy task to try to define what evil might be. Scholars in psychology, religious studies, neuroscience, philosophy, history, and other fields have come up with seemingly countless definitions that vary not only between, but also within, those fields.

On Defining Evil

Etymologically speaking, the word "evil" is considered to have developed from the Old English word, *yfel* and stems from Proto-Germanic *ubilaz* and serves as "the most comprehensive adjectival expression of disapproval, dislike or disparagement" (Harper, 2014, paras. 1–2). Anglo-Saxons used the word "evil" to refer to notions of "bad, cruel, unskillful, or defective," but as the language developed into Middle English, the word "bad" encompassed most of these ranges of meaning and "evil" was reserved for "moral badness" (Harper, 2014, para. 2). Although arguably we might dispute exactly what "bad" might mean, thinking about what leads someone to do "bad" deeds is even harder, and that is what concerns us in this book. How does evil happen? Who do we name as evil and why? And, why does it matter how we talk about evil?

If you are looking for a book that outlines one specific understanding of evil as the sole correct one, you have picked the wrong book. In fact, according to Alain Badiou (1993/2001), the imposition of a single truth is, in fact, a form of evil. Instead of arguing for a "best" definition of evil, I explain in this book that there are helpful (and harmful) definitions in a variety of contexts. What do I mean by helpful? I consider a definition of evil to be a helpful one if it opens up critical thinking, and thus a harmful definition as one that shuts down those higher-order thinking processes. In particular, I am concerned about our feelings of empowerment and agency, especially in relation to power structures. Although the definitions employed in this book vary greatly, there is a unifying theme that evil is not necessarily a tangible, physical, or spiritual *thing*; instead, evil is a *process* in the human realm. Evil "is not a character flaw that belongs to others, whether real or imagined, but rather a human quality" (Farley, 2009, p. 538; Stanley, 1999). I am purposefully not saying that evil is "controlled" by humans, even though it is tempting. My caution in the use of the word "control" is that humans can both intentionally and unintentionally commit evil, and when evil is unintentional, we can be completely oblivious to our wrongdoing. In that scenario, the evil-doer is not *in control* per se.

If provoking critical thought is the criteria, then a good definition of evil encourages *subjectification*, a term coined by Gert Biesta (2010) that describes the process of becoming a subject—how we "come to exist as subjects of initiative and responsibility rather than as objects of the actions of others" (Biesta, 2015, p. 77). Those acting as subjects possess the ability to think and act independently from authority but interconnected with others. Subjectification prevents us from being part of a mindless herd and instead invites us to think about how we might live together in good ways. In the context of education, subjectification might:

- encourage a sense of responsibility and agency in and out of the classroom;
- create educational contexts and systems that encourage genuine thinking; and
- live more peacefully and happily with each other (as well as other entities) on this planet.

4 C. van KESSEL

How we identify and define evil can help us subvert what we do not like about our societies, and this is an important initial step towards dismantling unhelpful structures and preventing unhelpful actions. A thoughtful consideration of evil can help this process, as opposed to a sort of "vulgar Manichaeism" where we might dismissively and simplistically name all that we "despise and want to destroy" as evil (Bernstein, 2002, p. 3).

Richard Bernstein (2002) has noted that in contemporary times the concept of evil has been used to stifle genuine thinking and public discussion, despite the discourse of evil having historically provoked inquiry in philosophy, religion, literature, and beyond. Of particular worry is the political employment of the word evil to sway public opinion; for example, George W. Bush used the word evil in over 800 speeches during his presidency (Barton, 2017). Arguably, such a political use of evil can serve to shut down critical thinking about government policies and actions (van Kessel, 2017). The goal of this book is to subvert such a process and those like it and instead provoke thinking *about* and *through* the concept of evil in the spirit of thoughtful education (as opposed to thoughtless schooling). I propose engaging with a variety of different definitions and exploring how they are helpful in specific contexts. But first, how has evil been taken up in educational research?

EVIL IN EDUCATIONAL RESEARCH

As a perennial concern throughout human history, there is much scholarly work on evil. This section, however, limited to a review of how the topic of evil has been examined in Anglophone educational research, with particular interest in the usage of the word and concept in social studies education spanning the years 1979 to present. I have not included my own publications that are referred to in the other chapters of this book. To ascertain the state of educational research on evil, I searched for the word "evil" in a variety of combinations with other words and phrases, including "social studies," "history," and "education" using the EBSCO Discovery Service (EDS) and Google Scholar. From the thousands of results, many authors employed the word "evil" as a descriptor or catchy title, rather than interrogating the actual topic of evil. For those who engaged with the idea of evil in the context of education, I noted those that: employed the label of evil, engaged with historical trauma, and reflected censorship and/or ideological schooling.

Most of the education-related scholarly works label historical events or figures as evil, and/or explore how we might teach evils as part of the curriculum (e.g., teaching about the Holocaust/Shoah).

Using the Label of Evil

There are some educational scholars have employed the word evil; however, the definition of evil is often not explicit. Rather, some sort of common understanding of evil is usually implicitly assumed; for example, Reis (2003) mentioned notions of combatting evil as the motivation for targeting women in the Salem witch trials. Because diagnosing evil is not the intention of the piece, it is logical that the topic is not engaged with thoroughly. Two studies in Anglophone educational research have involved students' views on evil. Neither of these, however, had evil as a main focus of study (i.e., the idea of evil was a taken-for-granted aspect of a broader worldview). Specific cultural value orientations affect a variety of attitudes, including those regarding human nature as evil, as evidenced by Carter, Yeh, and Mazzula (2008) in their study. The authors catalogued values and attitudes as well as the relationship between worldviews to five aspects of humanity: human nature, humans relating to the natural world, perspectives on time, human expression, and social relations. Mau and Pope-Davis (1993) noted, as part of their examination of the worldviews of students in counselling programs, that undergraduates were more likely than their graduate counterparts to perceive human nature as evil. This notion of human nature was only one of many questions posed to the students; other areas included the focus on the past, the nature of human relationships (linear vs. collateral and hierarchical vs. mutual), and the power of nature (Mau & Pope-Davis, 1993, p. 1).

Some educational scholars will intentionally employ the framing of good versus evil—not deconstructing the idea of evil, yet purposefully deploying the term. Egan (1979) incorporated emotional and moral confrontations between good and evil in his proposed first stage of social studies curriculum in which elementary students are in a mythic stage. Young children's minds, he argued, are easily engaged by stories of "witches, dragons, and talking animals in bizarre places and strange times" (Egan, 1979, p. 6), in part because these stories "are organized on those fundamental moral and emotional categories children know so clearly—love and hate, good and bad, fear and security, and so on" (p. 7). A minimal subjective interpretation of what might be good or evil

6   C. van KESSEL

is key because "young children require binary opposites" and "seem to grasp things initially in terms of polar opposites" before understanding nuances and middle ground (Egan, 1979, p. 8, 11). Thus, for practical reasons, Egan (1979) calls for an elementary curriculum that engages with a relatively simple understanding of evil. Another scholar who utilized a very particular conceptualization of evil purposefully is Parsons (1998). He called for the need to label and discuss historical evils in the context of social studies and religious education. Parsons (1998) provided a clear definition of evil as "a malicious disregard for others," and sees its presence in the reign of Saddam Hussein and in the lives of impoverished children (para. 7).

Just because the label of evil is not deconstructed does not mean that thoughtful discussions have not ensued. As an extended example, take Kevin Kumashiro's (2001) description of the Nazis as evil:

> ... the underlying story can change. For example, often absent from lessons on what many call the Second World War is any discussion of the role women played in transforming the workforce in the United States; of the persecution of queers in Nazi Germany alongside Jews and other targeted groups and of the forced relocation of Japanese Americans, many of them U.S. citizens, to internment camps primarily in the western United States. Such a unit indirectly tells a certain story about the way, something like the following: The Nazis were evil for persecuting the innocent Jews, the United States was the force of good in the face of this evil, the men in the United States helped save the world, and women/queers/Japanese Americans were not heroes, victims, or otherwise in this event. (p. 6)

Although the concept of evil itself is not explicitly troubled, such a framing implicitly questions the simplistic binary of good versus evil and invites us to consider our partial knowledge of the Second World War, among other catastrophes.

In drama, literature, social studies, and other courses, teachers and students explore historical and current events, as well as people, sometimes labelled as evil. The task of addressing the notion of evil is challenging. While evil is a familiar social signifier in politics and popular media, it is rarely defined. Philosophically speaking, there are numerous (and, at times, contradictory) definitions. Students' nascent understandings of evil, undoubtedly formed through many different influences, inform how they interpret historical and current events, and whether they see such events as inevitable, thus affecting their sense of future possibilities. Teachers might be reluctant to deconstruct the notion of evil for a variety of reasons; for example, they might want either to avoid conjuring up feelings of guilt or to maintain emotional distance from their students as a dispassionate expert delivering curriculum. Yet, some topics call upon teachers to think cautiously about how evil might be framed in their classrooms.

Evil and Historical Trauma

There is a responsibility to document and witness historical trauma such as the Vietnam War and the Holocaust/Shoah (e.g., Gaudelli, Crocco, & Hawkins, 2012; Simon, 2005; Simon & Eppert, 1997; Simon, Rosenberg, & Eppert, 2002). Learning about such events can be done in either a respectful or a disrespectful way, and thus, there are ethical obligations that arise from learning about the past through personal experience. Creating communities of remembrance through witnessing testimonies of social violence (i.e., evils) like genocide, colonialism, and slavery might help transform society by "affirm[ing] life in the face of death" (Simon & Eppert, 1997, p. 189). Pedagogy based on testimony and remembrance is a way of addressing evil in history through an understanding derived from Levinas:

> To speak to testimony means to attend to the limits displayed when recognition of another's experience lies in the mis-recognition of that experience as something one already knows. In the confrontation with such limits lies the possibility of experiencing what Levinas (1969) refers to as the "traumatism of astonishment" (p. 73), the experience of something absolutely foreign that may call into question what and how one knows. (Simon & Eppert, 1997, p. 180)

The ethical obligation then lies in working through the event in a self-reflexive way and in being attentive as both a judge and an apprentice (Simon & Eppert, 1997, p. 180). Encounters with traces of the past create opportunities to imagine a present and future potential of human society:

> While remembrance does not ensure anything, least of all justice, it can concretize human aspirations to make present a world yet to be realized,

thus present us with claims of justice and the requirements of compassion. (Simon, 2005, p. 102)

Roger Simon (2005) eloquently navigates an ethical response to evil by calling upon students and teachers to both witness and respond to historical trauma.

Timothy J. Stanley in his chapter, *A Letter to my Children: Historical Memory and the Silences of Childhood* (1999), describes his struggle to adequately respond to his children who ask him who the Nazis are. Simplistic binaries like those akin to "Manichean images of good and evil" (p. 39) are inadequate, and yet "Nazis are indeed bad guys" (p. 40). Drawing from Arendt's (1963/2006) idea of a banal evil (see Chapter 4), Stanley (1999) troubles the idea of a radical essence of evil in favour of a stance that implicates us all in our time, one that, interestingly, intentionally utilized the word "evil" and yet with the utmost thoughtfulness.

Lisa Farley and R. M. Kennedy also draw from Arendt, as well as psychoanalytic thinkers, in their article, *The Failure of Thought: Childhood and Evildoing in the Shadow of Traumatic Inheritance* (2017). Thinking is a dialogue with oneself and with others, and consequentially, such a task is "rooted in our earliest infantile experiences" (p. 123). Trauma, therefore, has a significant impact on our abilities to think and act in ethical ways. A failure to think (i.e., an Arendtian conceptualization of evil) is not that of an individual alone; rather, this failure also belongs to the social world.

Related to historical trauma is the practice of simulating tragic historical situations, some of which are often associated with a similar sense of the "evils" of the past, such as genocide and racism. Such simulations can be beneficial because they "enliven discussion of complex issues and perspectives, particularly around topics which may be difficult for students to grasp conceptually or empathetically through other means" (Wright-Maley, 2014, p. 18). Despite such potential benefits for understanding and engagement, the danger is that emotional trauma may result from simulations particularly if students are not properly prepared and debriefed, or the classroom atmosphere is not a safe space for emotions to be discussed, and/or parents are not informed about the simulation beforehand:

> Educators need to approach these activities with emotional and cultural sensitivity, be wary of early signs of psychological distress, have the tools to support students as they navigate any stress and strain they may feel, and know how to prepare both parents and students to make sense of the experiences before, throughout, and after the simulation is enacted. (Wright-Maley, 2014, p. 22)

Before any sensitive lesson is undertaken, simulation or not, care must be paid to what must happen before that lesson can occur; both intellectual and emotional needs must be anticipated.

Another concern about simulations is the potential to trivialize past horrors. Trotten and Feinberg (1995) examined Holocaust simulations and found the benefit of fostering empathy to be overshadowed by the cost of oversimplification of complex events. Wright-Maley (2014) acknowledges that concern as legitimate but adds that simulations can achieve a balance between gross oversimplification and confusing complexity in order to foster both empathy and learning (p. 20). In particular, the layer of morality in the simulation must remain complex, which can even help the students gain insight regardless of their prowess at the historical details (Schweber, 2003; Wright-Maley, 2014, p. 20). Approaches to the evils of history such as simulations—the Holocaust/Shoah, slavery, or other past horrors—have merit, but they must be implemented with care. Logistically, there are numerous concerns and there are no fewer emotional concerns. Linking back to the previous section on historical trauma, it behoves educators undertaking simulations to consider the ethical implications of witnessing and remembrance.

Censorship and Ideological Schooling

A variety of research exists that deals with the presence (or absence) of evil in school curricula. Marshall (2012) examined controversial content labelled as evil, namely the shift in the state policy of Victoria in Australia between the 1970s and the present regarding schools using books depicting homosexual behaviour. This debate was partly a response to fundamentalist Christian groups such as the Citizens Against Social Evil. Schools might censor material that influential and/or troublesome groups label as evil.

10   C. van KESSEL

An extension of censorship relates more directly to the teaching of history and involves issues of teaching contested or ideological history. Teaching history involves questions of the proper place of the ideological as it relates to political incantations of evil. According to Schär and Sperisen (2010), in Switzerland the political literacy of its population has changed along with the changing focus of the curriculum about the Second World War. These scholars examined the oscillating interpretations of the country's role in the Holocaust/Shoah from a neutral nation resisting evil to a complicit one faced with moral dilemmas. The concern for Schär and Sperisen (2010) lies in how historical memory is affected by the current political realm, particularly such a change in citizens' interpretation of their country's past from the immediate post-war narrative of resisting evil "prevent[ed] critical investigation into the nation's war history" to the new narrative highlighting "moral challenges" (Schär & Sperisen, 2010, p. 650). Evil (in this case, the narrative of a nation simply reacting to it) is deployed as a means to avoid more complicated historical realities. The assumption is that countries who examine the moral challenges faced by them as part of history education might be able to "combine their efforts to prevent such crimes in the future," but the aspect of agency discussed by the authors is that of those who teach contested history (Schär & Sperisen, 2010, p. 665).

In a U.S. context, Schrum (2007) examined ideological teachings present in higher education in the late 1930s as movements sought to inculcate the sense that the United States is a leader of the free world, particularly as a counterforce for evil dictatorships. Carlson (1985) examined a different era of ideological teachings, that of the Cold War. Carlson (1985), like Schär and Sperisen (2010), sees the semantic power of "evil" as preventing critical examination of history. He issues a strong critique of the simplistic and even misleading curricula about U.S.-Soviet relations in History textbooks for U.S. schools:

> Whether there is some validity to these charges [e.g., Communist plots for world domination] is not at issue here. What makes these texts primarily ideological is their intent to simplify and distort a complex situation since events are presented in an uncontested, taken-for-granted manner. (Carlson, 1985, p. 58)

There are educational scholars who have also made the opposite claim—that the United States needs more ideological teaching. In a more recent context,

Ravitch (2002) advocated for lessons about patriotism and recognizing the presence of evil in the post-9/11 world:

> Part of our postmodern view of the world has required us as educators to assert that good and evil are old-fashioned terms and somehow obsolete. We have now seen acts of wanton evil, akin to what earlier generations saw perpetuated by the Nazis and Communists... As educators, we have a responsibility to the public, to the children in our schools, and to the future. The public expects the schools to equip students with the tools to carry on our democracy and to improve it. (Ravitch, 2002, pp. 7–9)

Although Carlson (1985) and Ravitch (2002) disagree regarding their support for ideological teaching in U.S. schools, it is clear that both see the power of ideological teaching using the notion of evil. The naming and scope of ideological teaching are dependent on implicit assumptions about good and evil largely left in the realm of religion. Thus, questioning the idea of evil in a secular and educational setting offers a means to explore its ideological deployment more critically.

Ideological education can also take the form of character education for students (i.e., socializing them into the norms of their context). Gilead (2011) argued that this subject teaches more about virtues than vices, and thus, evil inclinations should be addressed more openly and fully. Moral education has come under criticism for its "inability to reduce violence, crime, abuse, vandalism, thievery and more... [and so] this has brought many to conclude that moral education must redirect its attention and focus on the development of moral character" (Gilead, 2011, p. 272). Aligning with Kantian ideas of radical evil, Gilead (2011) sees natural human inclinations such as "selfishness, cowardice, cruelty, envy, malice, jealousy... [as] the most controllable form of evil" (pp. 274–276), and so the evils of undeserved harm must be openly addressed in moral education in order for students to gain self-control. In a Russian context, Askarova (2007) argued that incorporating religious and ethical education encourages students to explore philosophy and their worldview more actively; for example, students and teachers should explore issues such as the nature and origins of good and evil with a view to "correcting" social and moral problems. Similarly, other scholars argue for the need to incorporate religious education in secular contexts in order to prepare students for dealing with the evils of the world, which might involve classifying evil (e.g., Miller, 1989).

12   C. van KESSEL

Regardless of a religious or secular framing, an element of ideological, values-laden education exists relative to the idea of evil.

The State of Educational Research on Evil

Overall, there is a distinct lack of research into students' conceptualizations of evil and the use of "evil" as a concept in classrooms, which is one of the reasons for the publication of this book. The research on historical trauma has provided valuable ways to refine our pedagogy based on a moral imperative to address the evils of history, while other research has illuminated issues of ideology and censorship on personal and systemic levels. Research thus far on personal views has been limited to broader categories such as human nature, rather than the nature of evil itself and its manifestations. I believe that it is critical to take educational research on evil further. My desire is that adding complexity to discussions of what we label as "evil" will contribute to more effective teaching and learning, as well as methods to help students cope with the difficult knowledge involved by refusing to let the word "evil" be used to shut down analysis and debate.

STRUCTURE OF THE BOOK

In Chapter 2, "Evil is in the Eye of the Beholder," I outline a few key themes that emerge from philosophical and psychological inquiries into evil. These examples illustrate key developments that have influenced the conceptualizations of evil I explore in subsequent chapters. I delve into Immanuel Kant's (1793/1838) understanding of a radical evil, which I juxtapose with the concept of *wétiko*, an idea present in several Indigenous cultures regarding the evil of a parasitic cannibal (e.g., Bouvier, 2018; Forbes, 1979/2008). These two examples are particularly pertinent regarding discussions about the extent to which intent is part of an evil act. The role of intent regarding an evil act as well as what evil might look like can be further dilated through particular figures from popular film and television: empathetic villains, anti-heroes, and domesticated evils.

In Chapter 3, "Banal Evil and Social Studies Education," I discuss Hannah Arendt's (1963/2006) idea of an ordinary evil. Her theory accounts for otherwise normal people who do not necessarily intend evil, but rather thoughtlessly perpetuate horrendous atrocities. With the help of Arendt's former student, Elizabeth Minnich (2014), I extend Arendt's line of thinking to the process of *villainification* (the creation of a single actor as the face of evil; van Kessel & Crowley, 2017), and thus, how we might normalize the villains of history in the hopes of recognizing (and preventing) similar evils from recurring.

In Chapter 4, "Processes of Evil as a Supplement to Citizenship Education," I engage with Alain Badiou's (1993/2001) understandings of evil as failures to uphold what might be good: betrayal, simulacrum/terror, and disaster. Rather than seeing citizenship as a set of skills to obtain, we might instead see a good citizen as one who can resist the processes that thwart our abilities to live harmoniously with others—to persevere in our goodness.

In Chapter 5, "The Politics of Evil," I outline one of the major findings from my doctoral work with Grade 11 students—the power of the word evil to stifle democratic debate while promoting hate speech. The word "evil" has immense power over our bodies and minds (Deleuze & Guattari, 1980/2008) and thus needs to be approached with caution, especially in the context of groups already marginalized.

In Chapter 6, "*Symbolic Evil* and the Schooling System," I discuss Jean Baudrillard's (1990/1993, 2004/2005) idea of *Symbolic Evil*. This particular form of evil is neither good nor bad in itself, but rather a force of radical change that we might judge later to be helpful or harmful. I argue that this conceptualization of evil can benefit our discussions of revolutionaries as well as schooling systems and other broad educational concerns like student success.

In Chapter 7, "Evil, Existential Terror, and Classroom Climate," I turn to the work of Ernest Becker (1973, 1975). Our fear of death that requires us to create anxiety buffers, like our cultural worldview. When we encounter those with different worldviews, we react as we would to any perceived threat to our lives: fight, flight, or freeze. Given that classrooms themselves can have a diversity of cultures and curriculum can conjure up divergent worldviews, knowledge of our threat and defence cycles can be a tool to help us encourage dialogue.

Throughout this book, I invite readers to consider evil not as a *thing* to behold, but an *invitation* to think about ourselves and our interconnectedness with others. Each understanding of evil offers an opportunity to (re)think aspects of education in and out of the classroom. Of course, each reader may connect with some conceptualizations more so than others, but key here is to ponder which ones are helpful in whatever areas of concern the reader has. Drawing from Nathan Snaza's (2014) article, "The Death of Curriculum Studies and its Ghosts," is my sincere hope that this book provokes thoughtful discussions about "experiment[s] with ways of being together as embodied beings caught up in educational sites that don't *hurt* quite so much, that produce unexpected by necessary *joys*" (p. 171).

REFERENCES

Arendt, H. (2006). *Eichmann in Jerusalem: A report on the banality of evil.* New York, NY: Penguin. (Original work published in 1963)

Askarova, G. B. (2007). The religious and ethical education of students in a secular school. *Russian Education and Society, 49*(1), 34–46.

Badiou, A. (2001). *Ethics: An essay on the understanding of evil* (P. Hallward, Trans.). London, UK: Verso. (Original work published in 1993)

Barton, R. (2017). Tribalism and the use of evil in modern politics. In M. Effron & B. Johnson (Eds.), *The function of evil across disciplinary contexts* (pp. 187–200). Lanham, MD: Lexington.

Baudrillard, J. (1993). *The transparency of evil* (J. Benedict, Trans.). London, UK: Verso. (Original work published in 1990)

Baudrillard, J. (2005). *The intelligence of evil or the lucidity pact* (C. Turner, Trans.). Oxford, UK: Berg. (Original work published in 2004)

Becker, E. (1973). *The denial of death.* New York, NY: Free Press.

Becker, E. (1975). *Escape from evil.* New York, NY: Free Press.

Bernstein, R. J. (2002). *Radical evil: A philosophical interrogation.* Cambridge, UK: Polity.

Biesta, G. (2010). *Good education in an age of measurement: Ethics politics, democracy.* Boulder, CO: Paradigm.

Biesta, G. (2015). What is education for? On good education, teacher judgement, and educational professionalism. *European Journal of Education, 50*(1), 75–87. https://doi.org/10.1111/ejed.12109.

Bouvier, V. (2018). Truthing: An ontology of living an ethic of *shakihi* (love) and *ikkimmapiiyipitsiin* (sanctified kindness). *Canadian Social Studies, 50,* 39–43.

Britzman, D. P. (1998). *Lost subjects, contested objects: Toward a psychoanalytic Inquiry of learning.* Albany: State University of New York Press.

Britzman, D. P. (2013). Between psychoanalysis and pedagogy: Scenes of rapprochement and alienation. *Curriculum Inquiry, 43*(1), 95–117. https://doi.org/10.1111/curi.12007.

Butler, J. (2004). *Precarious life: The powers of mourning and violence.* New York, NY: Verso.

Butler, J. (2009). *Frames of war: When is life grievable?* New York, NY: Verso.

Carlson, D. (1985). The Cold War in the curriculum. *Educational Leadership, 42*(8), 57–60.

Carter, R. T., Yeh, C. J., & Mazzula, S. L. (2008). Cultural values and racial identity statuses among Latino students: An exploratory investigation. *Hispanic Journal of Behavioral Sciences, 30*(1), 5–23. https://doi.org/10.1177/0739986307310505.

Deleuze, G., & Guattari, F. (2008). *A thousand plateaus: Capitalism and schizophrenia* (B. Massumi, Trans.). London, UK: Continuum. (Original work published in 1980)

Egan, K. (1979). *Individual development and the social studies curriculum* (ERIC No. ED183429). Paper presented at the Annual Meeting of the American Educational Research Association. San Francisco, CA.

Farley, L. (2009). Radical hope: Or, the problem of uncertainty in history education. *Curriculum Inquiry, 39,* 537–554.

Farley, L., & Kennedy, R. M. (2017). The failure of thought: Childhood and evildoing in the shadow of traumatic inheritance. *Review of Education, Pedagogy, and Cultural Studies, 39,* 121–138. https://doi.org/10.1080/10714413.2017.1296277.

Forbes, J. D. (2008). *Columbus and other cannibals.* New York, NY: Seven Stories. (Original work published in 1979)

Gaudelli, W., Crocco, M., & Hawkins, A. (2012). Documentaries, outtakes, and digital archives in teaching difficult knowledge and the Vietnam War. *Education & Society, 30*(2), 5–25. https://doi.org/10.7459/es/30.2.02.

Gilead, T. (2011). Countering the vices: On the neglected side of character education. *Studies in Philosophy and Education, 30*(3), 271–284. https://doi.org/10.1007/s11217-011-9223-1.

Hardy, T. (n.d.). *In tenebris II.* Retrieved from http://www.theotherpages.org/poems/hardy01.html.

Harper, D. (Ed.). (2014). Evil (adj). *Online Etymology Dictionary.* Retrieved from https://www.etymonline.com/word/evil.

Kant, I. (1838). *Religion within the boundary of pure reason* (J. W. Semple, Trans.). Edinburgh, Scotland: Thomas Clark. (Original work published in 1793)

Kumashiro, K. (2001). "Posts" perspectives on anti-oppressive education in social studies, English, mathematics, and science classrooms. *Educational Researcher, 30,* 3–12. https://doi.org/10.3102/0013189X030003003.

Lear, J. (2006). *Radical hope: Ethics in the face of cultural devastation.* Cambridge, MA: Harvard University Press.

Marshall, D. (2012). Historicizing sexualities education. *Review of Education, Pedagogy & Cultural Studies, 34*(1–2), 23–34. https://doi.org/10.1080/10714413.2012.643730.

Mau, W.-C., & Pope-Davis, D. B. (1993). Worldview differences between college students and graduate counseling trainees. *Counseling & Values, 38*(1), 42–50. https://doi.org/10.1002/j.2161-007X.1993.tb00819.x.

Miller, R. C. (1989). The problem of evil and religious education. *Religious Education, 84*(1), 5–15. https://doi.org/10.1080/0034408890840102.

Minnich, E. (2014). The evil of banality: Arendt revisited. *Arts & Humanities in Higher Education, 13,* 158–179. https://doi.org/10.1177/1474022213513543.

Parsons, J. (1998). Social studies and the problem of evil. *Canadian Social Studies, 33*(1), 14–16.

Ravitch, D. (2002). September 11: Seven Lessons for the Schools. *Educational Leadership, 60*(2), 6–9.

Reis, E. (2003). Confess or deny? What's a "witch" to do? *OAH Magazine of History, 17*(4), 11–15. https://doi.org/10.1093/maghis/17.4.11.

Ruti, M. (2017). The ethics of precarity: Judith Butler's reluctant universalism. In M. van Brever Donker, R. Truscott, G. Minkley, & P. Lalu (Eds.), *Remains of the social: Desiring the post-apartheid* (pp. 92–116). Johannesburg, South Africa: Wits University Press.

Schär, B. C., & Sperisen, V. (2010). Switzerland and the Holocaust: Teaching contested history. *Journal of Curriculum Studies, 42*(5), 649–669. https://doi.org/10.1080/00220271003698462.

Schrum, E. (2007). Establishing a democratic religion: Metaphysics and democracy in the debates over the President's Commission on Higher Education. *History of Education Quarterly, 47*(3), 277–301. https://doi.org/10.1111/j.1748-5959.2007.00101.x.

Schweber, S. A. (2003). Simulating survival. *Curriculum Inquiry, 33*(2), 139–188. https://doi.org/10.1111/1467-873X.00257.

Simon, R. (2005). *The touch of the past.* New York, NY: Palgrave Macmillan.

Simon, R., & Eppert, C. (1997). Remembering obligation: Pedagogy and the witnessing of testimony of historical trauma. *Canadian Journal of Education, 22*(2), 175–191.

Simon, R., Rosenberg, S., & Eppert, C. (2002). *Between hope and despair: Pedagogy and the remembrance of historical trauma.* Tampa: University of South Florida.

Snaza, N. (2014). The death of curriculum studies and its ghosts. *Journal of Curriculum and Pedagogy, 11,* 154–173. https://doi.org/10.1080/15505170.2014.966932.

Stanley, T. (1999). A letter to my children: Historical memory and the silences of childhood. In J. P. Robertson (Ed.), *Teaching for a tolerant world, grades K-6: Essays and resources* (pp. 34–44). Urbana, IL: National Council of Teachers.

Trotten, S., & Feinberg, S. (1995). *Diminishing the complexity and horror of the Holocaust: Lessons from classroom practice.* New York, NY: Teachers College Press.

van Kessel, C. (2017). A phenomenographic study of youth conceptualizations of evil: Order-words and the politics of evil. *Canadian Journal of Education, 40*(4), 576–602.

van Kessel, C., & Crowley, R. M. (2017). Villainification and evil in social studies education. *Theory & Research in Social Education, 95*(4), 427–455. https://doi.org/10.1080/00933104.2017.1285734.

Wright-Maley, C. (2014). In defense of simulating complex and tragic historical episodes: A measured response to the outcry over a New England slavery simulation. *Canadian Social Studies, 47*(1), 18–25.

CHAPTER 2

Evil Is in the Eye of the Beholder

It seems like there are countless definitions of evil, and so the goal of this chapter is not a comprehensive and broad survey. Instead, the purpose is to provide the reader with a sense of the possible tensions when trying to delineate what might be evil. Outlining a few significantly different ways of understanding evil serves as a springboard for more in-depth discussions in the following chapters. This chapter begins with a discussion of evil as a category of description, noting some of the variations possible. Next, I engage with Immanuel Kant's *radical evil* because it is an idea that has influenced many conceptualizations of evil over time. After Kant, I explore the concept of *wétiko* that is present in many Indigenous cultures. This conceptualization takes the idea of evil emphasizes an unnatural sickness of the soul, in contrast with a focus on specifically evil intent and actions. These two understandings—radical evil and *wétiko*—highlight how ideas about evil can diverge and yet each be helpful in their own way. In the latter part of this chapter, I examine how some popular film and television series can blur the distinction between good and evil, thus providing an opportunity to see evil on a spectrum rather than a specific category.

EVIL AS A CATEGORY

What is labelled as evil, and why? Interpretations of evil in philosophy have shifted significantly over the ages. Susan Neiman, a moral philosopher and cultural commentator, has traced the idea of evil over time.

© The Author(s) 2019

C. van Kessel, *An Education in 'Evil'*,

Palgrave Studies in Educational Futures,

https://doi.org/10.1007/978-3-030-16605-2_2

19

Neiman (2002) argued that the earthquake that destroyed Lisbon in 1755 literally and figuratively shook the previous foundation of a purely religious examination of evil—one that saw evil as God's way to good. Some, thus, began to differentiate between *natural evil* and *moral evil*, the former referring to misfortunes with no intent to harm (e.g., disease, earthquakes) and the latter referring to intentional and malevolent actions (Barton, 2017). After the Second World War, there was a renewed interest in evil as a label and a concept, understandably given the horrors associated with the war, particularly genocide. Terms other than evil—wrong, bad, and misfortune—seemed inadequate.

There are multiple ways to delineate different types of evil, perhaps in the hopes of understanding past evils and then subverting future ones. A philosopher of ethics and social philosophy, Claudia Card (2002), has reserved the label of evil only for large-scale atrocities (e.g., genocide, slavery, domestic abuse). By her definition, evils are foreseeable and committed by culpable wrongdoers. Similarly, but from a psychological perspective, Ervin Staub (1989) saw evil as extreme human destructiveness (e.g., genocide and mass killing), but later (2003) expanded his use of the word to extreme harm (e.g., pain, suffering, loss of life, or potential).

For some thinkers, they seek to provide a comprehensive description of the many misfortunes and ill deeds that might befall us, thus delineating multiple types of evil. One fruitful example is the work of Roger Shattuck (2001), a literary scholar, who identified four categories of evil:

- *natural evil*: elemental disasters and scourges (e.g., earthquakes, hurricanes, plagues). These occurrences are not the result of wrongdoing, neglect, or other culpable actions,
- *moral evil*: human actions that harm or exploit others, relative to morals of that society (e.g., murder, rape). These evils are ones that members of a society judge and punish accordingly, as well as try to prevent,
- *radical evil*: human actions that are so immoral that scruples and constraints are "utterly abandoned" (e.g., Marquis de Sade, Soviet Gulags, the Holocaust/Shoah)—evil that is "so extreme that it can no longer recognize its own atrocity" (p. 50), and
- *metaphysical evil*: when moral and/or radical evil become normalized as a sort of natural evil—when "the cruelest monsters and tyrants become normalized in the perspective of history and of 'the survival of the fittest' in evolution" (p. 50).

Regardless of whether we agree with Shattuck's (2001) particular categorization, it is clear that evil comes in many forms: intentional, premeditated, cruel, selfish, and among other characteristics. And, when considering human actions that are evil, the question arises: Why would someone commit evil? There are several strands of thought in this regard: action-based (e.g., some people are prone to evil and thus will do so on a regular basis), affect-based (e.g., some derive pleasure from inflicting harm), motivation-based (e.g., some have a propensity for desiring what will cause harm to others), and thus, there are some people who for one or more of these reasons commit evil (Calder, 2018). But why might we disregard the harm we might inflict upon others, whether that harm is pleasurable or more pragmatic? A significant thread in the conceptualization of evil over time has been the notion of a radical, a priori evil—an evil that exists in and of itself, as espoused by Immanuel Kant.

Immanuel Kant's Radical Evil

Kant, as part of the Enlightenment movement, did not seek to prove a transcendental evil within the confines of a religious orientation (e.g., he does not examine the Devil). According to Kant, evil is a rational choice freely made by humans—we know the right thing to do and yet do not follow it. He examined situations in which humans prioritize their natural desires over moral law (the categorical imperative). These natural desires are our self-love—we use our *subjective* reference point as an *objective* determining ground of a general will. Our experience is prioritized over that of others, and thus, we can easily fail to see the world from other perspectives and consequently deny others mutual recognition and respect. Philosophers such as Hegel and Schelling have responded directly to Kant's understanding of evil, and I recommend reading Richard Bernstein's (2002) commentary on that development.

Embedded in Kant (1793/1838) is an underlying pessimism. Humans have a propensity for self-love over moral law because we are sensuous creatures: "Every human, even the best" has this propensity for evil (6:36)—the privileging of our selfishness over everything else. He coined the term "radical evil" (*radikal Böse*) for this propensity (Bernstein, 2002, p. 5). Radical evil for Kant, thus, was not in the sense of being extreme; rather, it was radical because it is at the "root of human action, the fundamental choice of maxim that subsequently influences our choice of particular maxims" (Miller, 2015, p. 30). Evil is fundamental to our nature.

The Importance of Intent and Conscious Choices

For Kant, intent is what matters—our will, not our inclinations or even the deed itself. In short, if you do good things for immoral reasons, you are still evil. We can (and thus should) subvert evil:

> Reason tells us that we must follow the demands of reason and do our duty to others, whatever feelings or emotions of other non-moral incentives we may have to do otherwise. However, because we are free beings, we are not forced to follow the moral law, but can choose instead to follow those non-moral incentives. (Cole, 2006, p. 59)

Kant denied the possibility of good arising from anything non-rational. As such, if you help someone out of sympathy or empathy instead of a sense of duty, then you have committed a moral evil. He also does not think that evil can be done for evil's sake (i.e., evil will be committed for a reason related to our propensity for self-love).

It is important to be careful with words here. A "propensity" is deeper than an "inclination." Our propensity is for self-love, while our inclinations will be towards something more specific. Miller (2015) explained the difference between the two through the analogy of having an inclination towards lollipops because of a propensity for sweets (p. 41). According to Kant, all of us have a propensity for self-love, but we will vary to the degree we possess inclinations either to subordinate moral law to self-love or the opposite. As such, we are good or evil (but not both), depending on whether or not we subscribe to moral law. Despite this framing, we ought not to be taken Kant's idea of evil as simplistic. There are nuances within potential inclinations towards evil.

Someone may be inclined towards evil because of factors such as frailty, impurity, or perversity. *Frailty* indicates a weakness of will. People might be inclined towards evil because they cannot resist it (e.g., they cannot help themselves when they encounter a lollipop). We might also be inclined towards evil because of *impurity*—we might do the right thing but for the wrong reason (e.g., buying lollipops for a child not to make them happy, but so that you can justify having one, too). In this scenario, you might appear on the surface to be doing something good, but your motives lack the perspectives of others. That child may not want a lollipop; they might want something else, or perhaps they have diabetes and sugar will harm them. In my opinion, social justice work needs to beware of this form of evil. It is all too easy to make such work about yourself instead of those you claim to help. The third factor, *perversity*, is a selfish sort of wickedness to prioritize self-love over moral law (Kant, 1793/1838, 1:24–26). Perversity will result in wrongdoing when self-love conflicts with moral law, such as wanting so many lollipops that you demand more production from a factory reputed to have horrific working conditions due to the quest for maximum profit.

A Priori Evil vs. a Priori Good

One concern I have with Kant's emphasis on rationality is that he relies on the idea of conscious choice regarding an evil which naturally exists. Such a framing limits the possibilities for different (and more helpful) ways of being with each other in societies. According to Kant, we may not choose our propensity for good or evil, but we can control whether we act upon our inclinations. Humans can overcome evil through their attention to ethics based on rationality and moral law. In other words, evil exists as part of the natural order of things, and thus being good requires that we combat radical evil through adherence to an idealized rational morality. Evil exists a priori, and good only comes from responding to what is supposedly naturally there.

When I assess ideas of evil, I judge them based on what sort of thinking is opened up (or closed off) by them. In my opinion (and others may disagree), Kant's understanding of evil leaves few opportunities to imagine a different society. At best, we can manage what is innate to our being; there are limits based on the perception of our human nature. Some philosophers have flipped Kant's assumptions; for example, in Chapter 4, I explore Alain Badiou's (1993/2001) framing of a sort of a priori good (with evil existing only as a response to what might be good). For a more dramatic reimagining, however, it is important to move beyond Western European thinking.

The Evil of *Wétiko*

Jack D. Forbes (1979/2008), a professor emeritus and founder of the Native American Movement in 1961, wrote about the evil of *wétiko*—a cannibal. Although some of the stories are about cannibalism, other behaviours are also included, and instances of supposed cannibalism are perhaps metaphorical. It is important to note that a *wétiko* (when taken literally as a cannibal) devours others in a very hostile, disrespectful way, as opposed to particular consenting cannibals who eat their dead as a sign of respect (e.g., the Brazilian Wari). The precise meaning of *wétiko* will vary by context and the idea itself is complicated, but there are common threads that will inform my brief discussion in this section. Following Friedland (2018), I use the spelling "*wétiko*" because it mimics the Nehiyaw (i.e., Cree) pronunciation, but the word is sometimes spelled *witigo* (or other variants) and is referred to by other names in different cultures with their own variations in spelling, such as the *Chenoo* in Mi'kmaq, *windigo* in Ojibway, *wintiko* in Powhatan, and so on. The idea of a parasitic cannibal is evident in the thinking of a variety of groups in different geographical contexts, such as the Nehiyaw and Lakota Sioux of the North American plains as well as the Mbyá of central South America, among others.

In some traditions (e.g., Nehiyaw, Mi'kmaq), *wétikos* have hearts of hard ice, which has been interpreted literally by some (e.g., Cooper, 1933), but is more helpfully understood symbolically in relation to the cruel deeds of the *wétiko*. Both Forbes (1979/2008) and Friedland (2018) have engaged with *wétiko* behaviour beyond a simplistic account of literal cannibalism—the *wétiko* is a result of a sickness of exploitation that stands out from the goodness and love that is natural and normal. *Wétiko* behaviour is evident in how some corporate capitalists have controlled (gobbled up) the lives of their oppressed workers, how colonialists like Christopher Columbus have tried to absorb (guzzle) Indigenous peoples, as well as how Nazis murdered (consumed, and very literally processed) Jews, Romas, homosexuals, and others. *Wétikos* continually inflict harm upon others: "For the *wetiko* their insatiable appetite is never appeased and more importantly, there is no ethical boundary to which they abide" (Bouvier, 2018, p. 40). Despite falling into the trap of stereotyping Indigenous peoples, Morton Teicher (1960) nonetheless made the interesting observation that the *wétiko* is "perceived within culture as deviant from its norms… a clear and severe case of psycho-social dysfunctioning" (p. 5). Lou Marano (1982) rejected Teicher's idea of an individual psychosis and instead focused on group dynamics divorced from the cannibalistic elements, leading some to discount *wétikos* as just a story, while others (e.g., Brightman) placed the idea more helpfully within an Indigenous "context and cosmology" (Friedland, 2018, pp. 26–27).

In the sense of *wétiko*, evils are not simply a result of rational intentions or irrational accidents; they stem from "a genuine, very real epidemic sickness" and this "soul-sickness" is contagious (Forbes, 1979/2008, p. xviii). *Wétikos* recruit and corrupt others and also reproduce themselves by teaching others via education, various media, and institutional implicit and explicit training, such as "military training programs" and "high-pressure missionary groups" (Forbes, 1979/2008, p. 49). The *wétiko* disease is contagious and present in many facets of our lives: How we treat each other and the planet (Bouvier, 2018).

There are two key differences between Kant's view of evil and that of *wétiko*. The first difference is whether good or evil is considered to be the default. Forbes (1979/2008) identified love as the "norm" for humanity, with brutality as an "aberration" that is taught to us (p. 7), whereas Kant sees evil as natural and innate. Although Kant provides a framework to pursue the path of goodness, what hope is there if evil is the default? The second difference is the role of authenticity of those in society. Although Kantian and *wétiko* traditions are aligned with regard to the importance of intention and motivation, society can be structured in a way to encourage authenticity (or not). In either tradition, an evil-doer might choose to take advantage of others even while keeping up a façade of good, such as a violent racist attending a spiritual service that espouses goodness and peaceful relations. In both cases, the racist is clearly evil regardless of the façade. Yet, a society can be based on the sort of authenticity that prevents *wétiko* from pretending to be otherwise. Ceremonies in Indigenous traditions are meaningless without sincerity because of the belief that "one cannot fool the spiritual world by uttering words that contradict what is in one's heart, what one intends" (Forbes, 1979/2008, p. 58). A framing that emphasizes a priori good and a societal structure that requires authenticity strikes me as helpful as we seek the courage and resilience to counter the evils of the world.

A Spectrum of Evil in Popular Film and Television

Another helpful framing is to consider evil beyond a simple category, and certain depictions from film and television can assist in this task. In fact, when asking his introductory philosophy class about the nature of evil, Jamey Heit (2011) noticed that his students often referred to characters from popular media, such as Voldemort from the *Harry Potter* series (Rowling, 1997–2007) and Darth Vader from *Star Wars* (Kershner, 1980; Lucas, 1977; Marquand, 1983). The expanse of literature on evil in popular media is staggering, including its influence on youths, and thus, this section focuses on a specific question: What are some of the different ways in which evil is represented in popular media that challenge simplistic binaries of good and evil?

Media has the power to affect us, especially to open us up to others' ways of thinking (jagodzinski, 2014). In the context of evil, some film and television series can highlight the existence of a continuum of good and evil instead of an oppositional relationship. Three examples of such a continuum of evil are:

- evil characters with whom the audience can empathize,
- anti-heroes whose imperfections remind us of our own flaws, and
- domesticated evils that remind us of our own agency along that continuum.

These three variants of evil trouble Kant's dichotomy of being good or evil, thus providing us with an opportunity to broaden our perspective on human nature and society.

Empathetic Evil

What happens when we empathize with an evil character's motives? What if we understand why the villain does what they do, even if we disagree with the methods? Conventional evil narratives (i.e., those with obvious evil characters who are inevitably defeated) can still provoke meaningful questions about how we think about heroism and villainy (Forbes, 2011). In this sense, evil is still considered the antithesis of good, and yet evil is very meaningful. Two examples illustrate this complexity—The Joker from *The Dark Knight* (Nolan, 2008) and Erik "Killmonger" Stevens from *Black Panther* (Coogler, 2018).

In *The Dark Night*, the Joker is juxtaposed with Batman—both being neither wholly good nor evil. Although the narrative structure and genre lead us to expect (and hope for) the Joker to be defeated, we are invited to "reflect on ideas of values that we take for granted" (Forbes, 2011, p. 25). The Joker does not show the same simplicity that the other bad guys, the mobsters, seem to have. He does not want anything logical or predictable:

> *WAYNE/BATMAN*: "Criminals aren't complicated, Alfred. You just have to figure out what he's after."
> *ALFRED*: "With respect, sir, perhaps this is a man that you don't fully understand."

Bruce Wayne seems baffled that The Joker does not seem to be greedy. Alfred responds that The Joker's motivations were: "because he thought it was good sport. Because some men aren't looking for anything logical, like money. They can't be bought, bullied, reasoned, or negotiated with. Some men just want to watch the world burn." Such an observation solidifies the Joker as evil, mainly because he harms innocent people (e.g., willing to detonate a bomb in a hospital), but his sort of evil is more complicated than that. The Joker rejects the very heart of logic and reason— the sense that we can control the world around us. He even states: "I am not a schemer, I show the schemers how pathetic their attempts to control things really are." The Joker does not subscribe to the meaningless devotion to logic that permeates the surface of contemporary society:

> You see, their morals, their code, it's a bad joke. Dropped at the first sign of trouble. They're only as good as the world allows them to be. I'll show you. When the chips are down, these, these civilized people, they'll eat each other. See, I'm not a monster. I'm just ahead of the curve. (Nolan, 2008)

To an extent, the Joker is apt in his assessment, which challenges the audience to ponder their own beliefs about human nature and society. The culmination of this challenge is the climax of the film when the Joker sets up an experiment regarding human nature and instincts for self-preservation. He placed explosives on two ferries, one carrying prison inmates and their guards and the other with civilians and members of the National Guard. On each ferry is a detonator for the other ferry, placing those aboard in a precarious position. The Joker informs them that their ferry boat will remain intact if they blow up the other one and that they have until midnight or he will explode both of them. Any attempts to diffuse the explosives will also result in mutual destruction. The Joker expects that human nature will show its ugly side for self-preservation. However, something much more interesting unfolds. Our audience expectation might be that the prisoners would detonate the other bomb because they are assumed to already have some anti-social tendencies. The film itself leads us to this assumption as a large prisoner approaches a guard having trouble activating the detonator. Instead, the audience is might be surprised that the prisoner "does the right thing" and prevents anyone from detonating the explosives on the other ferry by throwing the detonator out the window. Also challenging our assumptions about human nature and who is "good" or "evil" is that the civilian and National Guard ferry boat passengers are much more eager to explode the prisoners. However, when the time comes to detonate, no one can actually go through with it. Now, the Joker's evilness becomes clear as his assumptions about human nature are defeated. He is an embodiment of pure anarchy, which can be thought of as an element inside us all the time that can manifest itself when we have the urge to question and rebel against structures. We might empathize with the Joker's frustrations with the world around him, but likely we disagree with how he seeks to destroy it.

Erik (Killmonger) from *Black Panther* (Coogler, 2018) is similar to the Joker in that we might identify with his concerns about society while condemning how he decides to act upon those concerns. Having grown up as not only an orphan but also subject to marginalization and oppression as a Black man in Oakland, California, he is understandably committed to freeing his people: "Two billion people all over the world who look like us, whose lives are much harder, and Wakanda has the tools to liberate them all!" That commitment is laudable, and yet "his traumatic loss of his entire family, his sense of moral obligation to a larger Black diasporic community of suffering—all morph into violent, short-sighted egotism and hyper-masculine megalomaniacal aggression" (Williams, 2018, p. 29). His methods are flawed, but his message is important. In fact, his message is so salient that some even question whether he is, in fact, a villain at all: "Killmonger is angry—not just at white supremacist oppressors or systemic racism, but also the Black Elite who left him behind. And he has every right to want vengeance" (Obie, 2018, para. 7).

Killmonger is a foil to King T'Challa of Wakanda in multiple ways. T-Challa seeks peaceful solutions, and thus, they stand in strong contrast in that regard, but importantly Killmonger reminds the audience that T'Challa and other Wakandans have neglected to act to help their kin in other parts of the world and instead have allowed oppression and genocide to flourish outside their boundaries. In fact, T'Challa's love, Nakia, had left him to help those outside Wakanda's borders, and yet he was still not moved to action until Killmonger arrived on the scene. Without Killmonger, would T'Challa have taken action to help the plight of Black folk worldwide? Given the plot of the film, this seems unlikely. If we ignore Killmonger's plans for world domination beyond liberation, and his disregard for the lives of his companion (e.g., his girlfriend whom he uses as a human shield), then, he seems more like a protagonist. T'Challa, however, reminds us of Killmonger's fatal flaw:

> T'CHALLA: You want to see us because just like the people you hate so much.
> KILLMONGER: I learn from my enemies!
> T'CHALLA: You have become them!

And this hypocrisy is why Killmonger remains the villain, despite his laudable goals. Here lies another complexity inherent in the film— violence itself is not demonized either:

> *Black Panther* does not render a verdict that violence is an unacceptable tool of black liberation—to the contrary, that is precisely how Wakanda is liberated. It renders a verdict on *imperialism* as a tool of black liberation, to say that the master's tools cannot dismantle the master's house. (Serwer, 2018, para. 12)

Killmonger's words and actions invite the audience to take a long, hard look at historical and contemporary oppression and its effects as well as their theories of how societal and political change happen. There are no easy answers to these provocations.

Both the Joker and Killmonger represent and embody particular aspects of society, but more importantly, they can function to provoke our own thinking about the world around us. Members of the audience might empathize with their perspective and thus feel uncomfortable and/or conflicted. Or, as especially seen in the case of *Black Panther*, even debate the extent to which the villain is, in fact, the bad guy. The opportunity for generating thought is boundless.

Anti-Heroes

Empathizing with a villain can generate thought, and similarly, when heroes are imperfect there is an opportunity to see a continuum of good and evil instead of a strict binary. Anti-heroes—protagonists who lack in their heroic qualities—can remind us of our own flaws and status as imperfect beings. Anti-heroes have existed in literature for some time, from ancient Greek tragedies to more contemporary works, including novels popular in English literature classes such as *L'Étranger* (*The Stranger/Outsider*) (1942) by Albert Camus. There seem to be countless anti-heroes in popular works including, but not limited to: Tyrion Lannister from George R. R. Martin's epic, *A Song of Ice and Fire* (1996–2011, now the popular *Game of Thrones* television series); Han Solo from *Star Wars* (Kershner, 1980; Lucas, 1977; Marquand, 1983); Daryl Dixon from *The Walking Dead* (Darabont, 2010–present); and Logan/Wolverine from *X-Men* (Donner, 2000–2017). All of these anti-heroes provide a means to challenge a simplistic delineation of good and evil, but for the sake of brevity, only one example will be explained in detail.

Some critics discard the character of Logan as a simplistic reproduction of white masculinity, but his status as a borderline character-in-flux reveals a much richer discussion (jagodzinski, 2014, p. 73). His flaws as an anti-hero are clear. In the first *X-Men* film (2000), he is an emotionally scarred loner whose allegiance to a cause or others is unsteady at best; for example, when he discovers Rogue stowing away in his vehicle, his first instinct is to leave her to the harsh elements, despite the fact that she might die from exposure to the cold.

In *X-Men* (2000), much time is spent "recruiting" Logan and attempting to make him a good guy. Professor Xavier bargains with him to help him discover his past in exchange for his allegiance. At the end of the film, however, Logan returns to his solitary life and continues his quest to find out about his origins. Logan's morality is also in question, as he actively pursues the love of Jean Grey, who is in a committed relationship with Scott. Logan's complexity as an anti-hero provides us with an example of someone who is imperfect, and yet we can still hope for his eventual victory and happiness. The audience is led by the narrative

2 EVIL IS IN THE EYE OF THE BEHOLDER   31

to root for him in his exploits, and yet he is far from a model for good behaviour and morality. These flaws make him more relatable. In his discussion of the heroification of historical figures, James Loewen (2007) noted that:

> when textbook authors leave out the warts, the problems, the unfortunate character traits, and the mistaken ideas, they reduce heroes from dramatic men and women to melodramatic stick figures. Their inner struggles disappear and they become goody-goody, not merely good. (p. 36)

Arguably, such portrayals alienate students from the figures they study—they cannot relate to them, and this situation is disempowering. Similarly, simplistic, "goody-goody" heroes are unrelatable due to their simplicity. Anti-heroes encourage the audience to see themselves and others as neither entirely good nor bad, and this spectrum stands in contrast with firm categories of evil.

Domesticated Evils

While meaningful, complex characters—both villains and anti-heroes—reveal a continuum between good and evil rather than a simple dichotomy, domesticated evils further blur the line by showing the softer side of evil. In other words, evil may not seem like evil at times. This form of enticing evil is most clearly seen in the contemporary vampire genre.

Historically, vampires have been alluring, but not domesticated. Characters like Lord Ruthven and Dracula clearly intended evil actions and their victims are random—anyone could be next, regardless of how innocent they are (Grant, 2011, p. 64). In "The Vampyre" (1819), a short story by J. W. Polidori, Lord Ruthven seduces women, murders them and (to the audience's horror) escapes unpunished. Bram Stoker's *Dracula* (1897) similarly shows a seductive vampire preying on the innocent, such as attacking the character, Mina, multiple times, and using his blood to control her for his own ends. It should be noted, however, that there are vampire characters from a range of time periods who are not alluring in any way. Both Count Orlok from *Nosferatu: A Symphony of Horror* (Dieckmann & Grau, 1922) and the Master from *Buffy the Vampire Slayer* (Whedon, 1997–2003) are not objects of desire because their "terrifying guise and anti-social nature make them unconducive to romantic discussion" (Ndalianis, 2012, p. 90). Orlok and the Master

32   C. van KESSEL

remain more one-dimensional as antagonists than vampires like Ruthven or Dracula.

In the twentieth century and beyond, domesticated vampires have appeared in works like Stephanie Meyer's *Twilight* Saga (2005–2008). Plots like that of *Twilight* have human women falling in love with vampires, thus blurring the boundaries between good and evil even further as the romantic vampires become objects of sympathy as well as desire in popular consciousness (Anastasiu, 2011). The young male vampire protagonist, Edward Cullen, shows affection and kindness to his human love, Bella, and yet he has his dark side, including acts of revenge and murder. Despite his technical monster status, Edward has both a good and evil side and resembles humans in both appearance and rationality. The world of vampires in *Twilight* is one in which blood substitutions (animal for human) are possible and vampires can choose to live as a loving family.

No one, not even the undead, is evil by nature; rather, both human and vampire can choose to be good or evil (Grant, 2011). Evil in *Twilight* takes two forms: vampires who disregard the laws and those who desire power. Nomadic vampires like Laurent, James, and Victoria are portrayed as "mere animals of instinct" and "slaves to their dark passions" (Grant, 2011, p. 74). Here, the simplistic colonial binary of "civilized" and "uncivilized" appears. The untamed wildness of these three vampires is contrasted with the domesticated family of the Cullens. While the Cullens seem fully "house-trained" with their respect for family and the laws of both the human and vampire world, the nomads shirk all of these responsibilities by hunting in others' territory and killing without thought. In a few senses, these nomads resemble the nineteenth-century vampires with their disregard for their victims. However, there is no religious element or determinism. These vampires have clearly chosen the wrong path when other options were available to them. Dracula, however, had no other option but his demise if he were to refuse human blood. In *Twilight*, there is not much blurring between good and evil, but rather a redefinition of who is good or evil; e.g., criminals and miscreants are still seen as worthy of death. Nonetheless, such paranormal romance narratives, including the somewhat simplistic *Twilight* saga, make possible "the exploration of social boundaries relating to sex, passion and desire" (Ndalianis, 2012, p. 91), and I would argue the nature of evil as well.

A Range of Evil

Creating categories of evil is no easy task—philosophers, psychologists, social theorists, theologians, and many others working in a variety of disciplines have understandably wrestled with the idea of evil. Although attempts have been made to delineate what evil can be (and, in some cases, postulate subtypes), in the end the topic of evil begs the question: *What might the study of evil illuminate about our past, present, and future possibilities for living together on this planet?* As such, the study of evil is part of what Todd May (2005) sees as the primary question of philosophy: "How might one live?" (p. 1). The concept of *wétiko* invites community members to consider how they relate to each other and other entities on the planet: How might we live *together?* Kant sought to create universal rules by which to answer a similar question, but with defined answers and rules instead of the more general disposition that we can learn from the destructive example of the *wétiko*. Empathetic villains, anti-heroes, and domesticated evils defy simple categorization, and thus invite us to see the murky ethical spaces in between good and evil. In these ways, identifying what exactly evil is becomes less of a priority than how evil functions—and thus how we, as human individuals interconnected in societies, might live in less harmful ways together.

References

Anastasiu, H. (2011). Someday my vampire will come? Society's (and the media's) lovesick infatuation with prince-like vampires. In M. Parke & N. Wilson (Eds.), *Theorizing Twilight: Critical essays on what's at stake in a post-vampire world* (pp. 41–55). Jefferson, NC: McFarland & Company.

Badiou, A. (2001). *Ethics: An essay on the understanding of evil* (P. Hallward, Trans.). London, UK: Verso. (Original work published in 1993)

Barton, R. (2017). Tribalism and the use of evil in modern politics. In M. Effron & B. Johnson (Eds.), *The function of evil across disciplinary contexts* (pp. 187–200). London, UK: Lexington.

Bernstein, R. J. (2002). *Radical evil: A philosophical interrogation.* Cambridge, UK: Polity Press.

Bouvier, V. (2018). Truthing: An ontology of living an ethic of *shakihi* (love) and *ikkimmapiiyipitsiin* (sanctified kindness). *Canadian Social Studies, 50,* 39–43.

Calder, T. (2018). The concept of evil. In E. N. Zala (Ed.), *The Stanford Encyclopedia of Philosophy* (Fall 2018 Edition). Retrieved from https://plato.stanford.edu/archives/fall2018/entries/concept-evil/.

34   C. van KESSEL

Camus, A. (1982). *The stranger* (K. Griffith, Trans.). Washington, DC: University Press of America. (Original work published in 1942)

Card, C. (2002). *The atrocity paradigm: A theory of evil.* New York, NY: Oxford University Press.

Cole, P. (2006). *The myth of evil: Demonizing the enemy.* Edinburgh, Scotland: Edinburgh University Press.

Coogler, R. (Director). (2018). *Black Panther* [Motion picture]. USA: Walt Disney.

Cooper, J. M. (1933). The Cree Witiko psychosis. *Primitive Man, 6*(1), 20–24.

Darabont, F., et al. (Producers). (2010–present). *The walking dead* [Television series]. New York, NY: AMC.

Dieckmann, E., & Grau, A. (Producers), & Murneau, F. W. (1922). *Nosferatu: A symphony of horror* [Motion picture]. Weimar Republic: Film Arts Guild.

Donner, L. S. (Producer). (2000–2017). *X-Men* [Motion picture series]. USA: 20th Century Fox.

Forbes, D. A. (2011). The aesthetic of evil. In J. Heit (Ed.), *Vader, Voldemort and other villains: Essays on evil in popular media* (pp. 13–27). Jefferson, NC: McFarland & Company.

Forbes, J. D. (2008). *Columbus and other cannibals.* New York, NY: Seven Stories. (Original work published in 1979)

Friedland, H. L. (2018). *The Wetiko legal principles: Cree and Anishinabek responses to violence and victimization.* Toronto, ON: University of Toronto Press.

Grant, A. J. (2011). Focus on the family: Good and evil vampires in the Twilight Saga. In J. Heit (Ed.), *Vader, Voldemort and other villains: Essays on evil in popular media* (pp. 64–79). Jefferson, NC: McFarland & Company.

Heit, J. (2011). Preface and introduction. In J. Heit (Ed.), *Vader, Voldemort and other villains: Essays on evil in popular media* (pp. 1–11). Jefferson, NC: McFarland & Company.

jagodzinski, j. (2014). Pedagogy in the public realm: Affective diagrams of thinking feeling in the X-Men and beyond. In J. Burdick, J. A. Sandlin, & M. P. O'Malley (Eds.), *Problematizing public pedagogy* (pp. 65–75). New York, NY: Routledge.

Kant, I. (1838). *Religion within the boundary of pure reason* (J. W. Semple, Trans.). Edinburgh, UK: Thomas Clark. (Original work published in 1793)

Kershner, I. (Director). (1980). *The empire strikes back* [Motion picture]. USA: 20th Century Fox.

Loewen, J. W. (2007). *Lies my teacher told me: Everything your American history textbook got wrong.* New York, NY: Simon & Schuster.

Lucas, G. (Director). (1977). *Star wars: A new hope* [Motion picture]. USA: 20th Century Fox.

Marano, L., et al. (1982). Windigo psychosis: The Anatomy of an emic-etic confusion [and comments and reply]. *Current Anthropology, 23,* 385–412.

Marquand, R. (Director). (1983). *Return of the Jedi* [Motion picture]. USA: 20th Century Fox.

Martin, G. R. R. (1996–2011). *A song of ice and fire.* New York, NY: Bantam.

May, T. (2005). *Gilles Deleuze: An introduction.* Cambridge, UK: Cambridge University Press.

Meyer, S. (2005–2008). *The Twilight Saga* [Novel series]. New York, NY: Little, Brown.

Miller, E. N. (2015). *Kant's religion within the boundaries of mere reason.* London, UK: Bloomsbury.

Ndalianis, A. (2012). *The horror sensorium.* Jefferson, NC: McFarland & Company.

Neiman, S. (2002). *Evil in modern thought.* Princeton, NJ: Princeton University Press.

Nolan, C. (Director). (2008). *The dark knight* [Motion picture]. USA: Warner Bros.

Obie, B. (2018, February 17). In defense of Erik Killmonger and the forgotten children of Wakanda. *Shadow and Act.* Retrieved from https://shadowandact.com/erik-killmonger-forgotten-wakanda.

Polidori, J. W. (1819). *The Vampyre.* London, UK: Sherwood, Neely, and Jones.

Rowling, J. K. (1997–2007). *Harry Potter* [Novel series]. New York, NY: Arthur A. Levine.

Serwer, A. (2018, February 21). The tragedy of Erik Killmonger: The revolutionary ideals of Black Panther's profound and complex villain have been twisted into a desire for hegemony. *The Atlantic.* Retrieved from https://www.theatlantic.com/entertainment/archive/2018/02/black-panther-erik-killmonger/553805/.

Shattuck, R. (2001). Narrating evil: Great faults and "splendidly wicked people". In J. L. Geddes (Ed.), *Evil after postmodernism: Histories, narratives, and ethics* (pp. 45–55). New York, NY: Routledge.

Staub, E. (1989). *The roots of evil: The origins of genocide and other group violence.* New York, NY: Cambridge University Press.

Staub, E. (2003). *The psychology of good and evil: Why children, adults, and groups help and harm others.* Cambridge, UK: University of Cambridge Press.

Stoker, B. (1897). *Dracula.* Edinburgh, UK: Archibald Constable and Co.

Teicher, M. I. (1960). *Windigo psychosis: A study of a relationship between belief and behavior among the Indians of Northeastern Canada.* Seattle: WA: American Ethnological Society.

Whedon, J. (Producer). (1997–2003). *Buffy the Vampire Slayer* [Television series]. Hollywood, CA: Warner Bros.

Williams, D. (2018, August). Three theses about Black Panther. *The Journal of Pan African Studies, 11*(9), 27–30. Retrieved from http://www.jpanafrican.org/docs/vol11no9/11.9-special-5-Williams.pdf.

CHAPTER 3

Banal Evil and Social Studies Education

One of the most uncomfortable realizations about evil is that it can be part of our daily lives. Evil in this chapter is examined in its form as large-scale violence (e.g., genocide, racism). It is easy for us to assume that atrocities are reserved for far-away places or strangers in the distant past, but such assumptions would be incorrect. Evil comes in many forms; some evildoers are extraordinary while others are not. Hannah Arendt (1906–1975) helps us think through evil when terrible deeds are perpetuated not by unique individuals (e.g., serial killers), but by ordinary people.

HANNAH ARENDT

Arendt was a German philosopher of Russian-Jewish ancestry. In 1941, as Nazi aggression engulfed Europe, Arendt made her way to the United States. Her scholarship, in part, reflected her wartime experiences and her resulting commitment to understand human capacities for evil. In her early work, Arendt employed a conceptualization of radical evil; however, after witnessing the trial of Adolf Eichmann, Arendt engaged with a different understanding—the *banality of evil*. This shift in focus from an extraordinary to ordinary sense of evil reveals a provoking way of thinking and teaching about the horrors of the past and present.

© The Author(s) 2019

C. van Kessel, *An Education in 'Evil'*,

Palgrave Studies in Educational Futures,

https://doi.org/10.1007/978-3-030-16605-2_3

38   C. van KESSEL

After outlining Arendt's theories of evil, and the work of her former student, Elizabeth Minnich (2014), I will map out a process called *villainification*: the creation of a single actor as the face of evil (van Kessel & Crowley, 2017; van Kessel & Plots, in press). Anti-villainification education allows for the teaching and learning of historical and contemporary events in ways that do not simplistically blame either one person or the amorphous entity that is "society." Avoiding these framings is important because they (often unintentionally) absolving us all from responsibility; therefore, we need ways of thinking about these evils with more complexity, and Arendt is helpful in this regard.

RADICAL EVIL

In *The Origins of Totalitarianism* (1951/1966), Arendt articulated her belief in a radical evil: "We may say that radical evil has emerged in connection with a system in which all men [sic] have become equally superfluous" (p. 459). Such a claim likely arose from the influence of the two World Wars, during which millions of people were "treated as if they were completely dispensable" (Bernstein, 2002, p. 19). These wars saw soldiers treated like pawns, civilians rendered homeless and stateless, not to mention the millions of Jews, Roma, homosexuals, as well as people with physical and mental disabilities, dehumanized completely and murdered on a massive scale by the Nazis in the Second World War. Although Kant (1793/1838) coined the term "radical evil" to describe human selfishness in contrast with adherence to moral law, Arendt (1951/1966) sees such an evil as beyond the human scale. This understanding led Arendt to an interpretation that the Nazis were conduits for an absolute evil force:

> Totalitarian regimes have discovered without knowing it that there are crimes which men [sic] can neither punish nor forgive. When the impossible became possible it became the unpunishable, unforgivable absolute evil. (Arendt, 1951/1966, p. 459)

This evil was what "corrupted the basis of moral law, exploded legal categories, and defied human judgment" (Elon, 2006, p. xiii) and in this sense becomes *beyond* human. Although radical evil was a productive line of thinking at the time, Arendt later came to see another manifestation of evil—equally horrific, but overwhelmingly ordinary.

THE BANALITY OF GOOD AND EVIL

I see Arendt's banality of evil as arising, in part, as a complement to her earlier conception of a banal sense of good. In Arendt's early work, she saw evil as radical, but goodness was in the domain of ordinary humans. In *The Human Condition* (1958/1998), Arendt articulated the idea of *action*, which spoke to the ordinary qualities that our supposed heroes possess: no special powers, status, or genealogy are required. Following ancient Greek thought, a hero needs no "heroic" qualities per se; the word "hero" as it appears in Homer's *Iliad* was no more than a term given to those who participated in the Trojan enterprise (p. 186). Although anyone is technically capable of *action*, not everyone will take it.

Taking *action* necessitates ordinary people working collectively to make the world into a place suitable in which to dwell; it creates relationships as it shatters limitations and boundaries, which is why the *polis* is not really a city state but rather the connections among the people resulting from their *actions* (Arendt, 1958/1998, pp. 190 and 198). What is necessary for public thinking, and this *action*, is a sense of interconnection among us. For Arendt, *action* referred to a conception of politics based on a capacity to do the unexpected—humans have the potential to alter their existence in meaningful ways. In order to take *action* in this sense, humans must think independently from authority while thinking interdependently with others, and every one of us has this capacity.

Ordinary People and Evil

Having already articulated the idea of the ability for ordinary folks to contribute in heroic ways, Arendt (1963/2006) went on to reveal the mundane characteristics of villains in her book, *Eichmann in Jerusalem: A Report on the Banality of Evil*. She challenged what had been commonly accepted at the time both morally and legally: "namely, that people who do evil deeds must have evil motives and intentions" (Bernstein, 2005, p. 7).

If not an intent to harm, what begins the process of evil? For Arendt (1963/2006), this evil is a form of thoughtlessness—not only a lack of thinking per se (i.e., mindlessly following orders), but also, more disturbingly, a lack of critical thought about how an individual can affect others.

It should be noted that for Arendt (1963/2006), evil itself is not ordinary; for example, the Holocaust was unique in its horror and Arendt does not ignore the gravity of such atrocities. However, such extraordinary evils are a product of the interconnected deeds of ordinary people, not limited to a single maniacal villain. The banality of evil does not mean that evil is an everyday occurrence, but rather:

> the phenomenon of evil deeds, committed on a gigantic scale, which could not be traced to any particularity of wickedness, pathology, or ideological conviction in the doer, whose only personal distinction was perhaps extraordinary shallowness... However monstrous the deeds were, the doer was neither monstrous nor demonic... [Evil] can spread over the whole world like a fungus and lay waste precisely because it is not rooted anywhere. (Novick, 1999, p. 135)

For Arendt, evil is not only organized violence against targeted people, but also the bureaucratic and banal "non-thinking" routines that underlie such violence. This non-thinking is not stupidity, but rather thoughtlessness. Our English word, "idiot," comes from the Greek word for "private person," a person who is not working towards the greater good of the state (Liddell & Scott, 1996, p. 819). Here, the "state" refers to the Greek *polis*, which is a composite of the interconnected citizenry, not simply the government or the physical land per se. It is important to note here that there cannot be an arbitrary definition of the public (e.g., the Nazis decided that the only "public" who mattered were Aryans); rather, the public ought to be understood as all of those with whom we are interconnected. This sort of idiocy entails that folks think only of their own private concerns and do not think of the harm they inflict upon others in their immediate community and beyond.

This situation of non-thinking is sometimes explored in the context of claims of just following orders, as in Stanley Milgram's (in)famous experiments on destructive obedience as well as the My Lai Massacre trials during the Vietnam War (e.g., Mann, 1973). In the early 1960s at Yale, Milgram conducted a study in which participants were told to administer increasingly powerful electric shocks as a teaching tool on another "participant" (who was part of the research team, and not a participant per se). Also unbeknownst to the participants was that no shocks were actually administered. Milgram conducted this study because of a similar concern that Arendt had noticed: Why do people follow orders to harm and kill, such as during the Holocaust? Milgram (1963) noted:

> Gas chambers were built, death camps were guarded, daily quotas of corpses were produced with the same efficiency as the manufacture of appliances. These inhumane policies may have originated in the mind of a single person, but they could only be carried out on a massive scale if a very large number of persons obeyed orders. (p. 371)

Milgram's study and others that have followed prompt discussion about obedience. Some people act as if they have no choice but to obey an authority figure (Hamachek, 1976). Participants in Milgram's study who completed the experiment and issued the maximum levels of electric shocks seemed to deflect responsibility to the experimenter: "You [the experimenter] want me to keep going?" "You accept all responsibility?" "You're going to keep giving him, what, 450 volts?" (Matt, 2013). Such sentiments stand in contrast with participants who disobeyed orders: "Take the cheque back. I'm not going to hurt the guy!" "Yes, I have a choice!" (Matt, 2013). Hamachek (1976) noted that "The most disturbing phenomenon is that so many of us seem to behave as if we are robbed of free will once a directive is issued from a sufficiently powerful authority source" (p. 444). Regardless of whether someone is following orders or simply failing to consider how their actions affect others, the evil they are part of is a form of thoughtlessness.

The Wrong Man for a Good Theory

Arendt's banality of evil as thoughtlessness was inspired by her observations of Adolf Eichmann, a Nazi logistical manager whose facilitation of the Holocaust contributed to millions of deaths. He had escaped prosecution for his war crimes until 1960, when Israeli secret service officers captured him and brought him to Israel. Arendt covered his trial for *The New Yorker*, and her book is a revised collection of these articles.

During the trial, Eichmann claimed that he was merely a bureaucrat who was following orders. His appearance in court did not reflect assumptions about how a villain should look—he was old, he had thick glasses, and he even was suffering from a cold. This unassuming, even seemingly weak, human was not what Arendt expected. Eichmann was far from a demonic monster. From the testimony, he seemed like a "drab drone committed to industriousness and efficiency, a featureless functionary particularly steadfast in obeying and carrying out assigned duties" (Waller, 2007, p. 100).

As it turns out, Arendt chose a poor example of an otherwise important concept. Notable historians have refuted Eichmann's testimony about his intentions (e.g., Stangneth, 2015). Arendt was duped by Eichmann's claims that he lacked evil intent, but such a ruse was only possible because there were indeed "so many perpetrators of the kind he was pretending to be" (Browning, 2003, pp. 3–4). Browning (1993) has provided better examples of the banality of evil through an examination of the transformation of the regular men of the Order Police into brutal killers in the 1930s. Eichmann himself is perhaps better understood in the context of ordinary people's propensity for fetishizing evil—still an ordinary person, but one who comes to delight in the harm they cause (van Kessel, 2018).

Regardless of Eichmann's character, there were ordinary humans, not unlike us, who took part in the genocide in Nazi Germany. The Holocaust/Shoah happened, in part, because of the:

> nature of the bureaucratic mind—a world of operations without consequences, information without knowledge: in other words, mindless perpetrators doing what they are ordered to do and expected to do without being personally involved, committed, or aware of the terrifying destruction they are executing. (Waller, 2007, p. 100)

Such a process would also hold for the Rwandan and Bosnian genocides in the 1990s, among others. Those who instigated, perpetuated, and facilitated atrocities were many, and not all of them intended to inflict the harm that they did. While some were eager, others needed to be coaxed or coerced, and some did not think about their actions at all (Hatzfeld, 2006).

Intensive and Extensive Evil

Partially in response to the criticisms of Arendt, Elizabeth Minnich (2014) broke down evil into two categories—*intensive* and *extensive*, the latter of which is a reformulation of Arendt's banality of evil. *Intensive* evils are massive in scale and perpetuated by a limited number of people who "stand in shuddering contrast with the lives others are leading around them in their times. When they burst into our lives, we are genuinely spectators, not participants, not enablers, and not perpetrators" (Minnich, 2014, p. 169). An example of this sort of evil would be psychopathic mass murderers. Intensive evils are neither systemic nor thoughtless and thus are "precisely not ordinary" (Minnich, 2014, p. 169). In contrast with intensive evils, *extensive* evils are:

> the massive and monstrous harms carried out by many, many people for significant periods of times—months, years, decades, and more (slavery and sexualized violence: when has humanity been without these and others?). They are the evils of which we would not speak, of which we so often say, "unthinkable." (Minnich, 2014, p. 170)

Ordinary people considered to be decent citizens perpetuate extensive evils and the systemic level of the evil requires that sustaining it "be conventional to do its work as one's job, daily, day after day after day after day, with supper at home and picnics on the weekends" (Minnich, 2014, p. 170). Extensive evils would include the harmful, widespread, and institutional practices of Indian Residential Schools in the United States and Canada, which involved government officials forcibly removing Indigenous children from their homes and placing them in boarding schools to assimilate them into White cultural norms (and where these children faced emotional, physical, and sexual abuse).

It is easy to be horrified by intensive evils. Extensive evils, however, are complex, nuanced, and even subtle at times, and, due to a necessarily broader assessment of culpability, can be threatening to us personally as well as to our worldview (for an exploration of worldview threat, see Chapter 7). Such a threat can force a sort of non-thinking, or even simple thoughtlessness—as Alan Harrington (1969) stated, an "inertia of neglecting to feel" (p. 153).

Villainification

The process of villainification is the creation of a single actor who becomes the face of an extensive evil (van Kessel & Crowley, 2017). There is a tendency to simplify what is labelled as evil in historical as well as in contemporary events, shifting the focus from the systemic and ordinary to the extraordinary hyperindividual. The villains of history become devoid of normal, ordinary characteristics as the focus is shifted to their evil deeds and inclinations. This lack of thinking about how we might be personally implicated in systemic harm then provides the opportunity to shirk responsibility, such as ascribing racism just to individuals like David Duke, the former Grand Wizard of the Ku Klux Klan, and thus failing to see how many of us inadvertently prop up white supremacy through our hiring practices, school choices, social circles, preconceived notions about students of colour, and so on.

Villainification is a parallel but opposite process to heroification, the creation of larger-than-life heroes in history (Loewen, 2007). Heroification obscures how ordinary people and processes shape our world. Teachers and textbook writers may craft heroification narratives to provide inspiration for students, but ironically these narratives can also cause disengagement by turning "flesh-and-blood individuals into pious, perfect creatures without conflicts, pain, credibility, or human interest" (Loewen, 2007, p. 11). Heroification can stifle students' feelings of civic agency and self-efficacy (Epstein, 1994) by minimizing the importance of communities that mobilize to create social change (e.g., Alridge, 2006; Kohl, 1991; Woodson, 2016).

Ultimately, heroification and villainification narratives transmit similar lessons: we inaccurately learn that social change occurs through the intentions and deeds of extraordinary individuals. Both processes boil down intricate webs of events, people, and ideologies into an essentialized, isolated component—the single actor. While curricular representations of heroification and villainification share some of the same shortcomings, villainification narratives (and the conceptualization of individualized evil they promote) arguably do greater harm. By oversimplifying and over-individualizing certain types of evil, villainification obscures our understanding of how we perpetuate evil through our daily actions. Despite the scope of extensive evils such as racism, we tend to interpret the consequences of ill intent as being "in the heart of particularly evil individuals" instead of in the heart of society (Coates, 2013, para. 6). There is a need to examine both—the broader system as well as the individuals working within that system. Such an examination needs to be done without absolving those who comprise this system of their responsibility, regardless of whether they are aware of their complicity.

The task of anti-villainification, in part, removes our false sense of comfort that evil is other, and not us. We are called upon us to engage with a more complete analysis of historical actors and contingencies, with an emphasis on the critical reflection about the ways that ordinary situations and people in our own lives, including ourselves, reproduce injustice.

Meaningful Complexity

How we study the processes of history affects our sense of agency in the here and now; student reflection upon ethical concerns in the past "sensitize[s] the students to the predicament of ethical-political choices that they, as citizens, must face today" (Löfström, 2013, p. 517; Selman & Barr, 2009). Such a process of sensitization entails that we cannot consider individuals as simplistic villains because then we can thoughtlessly discard them as aberrant without further thought. Aristotle, in his *Poetics*, sees the function of tragedy as to arouse pity and fear because the characters display a universal human vulnerability to tragic events. The characters are realistic in that they are neither purely virtuous nor wicked and thus make an error (*hamartia*) as opposed to a purposeful action out of evil intention (Aristotle, 335 B.C.E./1995). If this complexity is removed, then the audience's ability to feel the weight of the tragedy is stunted. By extension, curriculum (including textbooks) can remove students' (and teachers') ability to relate to the historical figures they study. It is not merely the information about nuanced characters; there is a necessity to feel at least somewhat uncomfortable that the perpetrator of the evil deed is a fellow human just like you and those in your life.

The Banality of Evil and Villainification

Arendt and Minnich articulated that many of those involved in extensive, banal evils would be considered in other context to be "normal" people in terms of their morality and demeanour. Their analysis points to the danger of villainification narratives in highlighting individual actions and obscuring the thoughtlessness (and thus complicity) embedded in the everyday actions of ordinary folks. The lack of monstrosity required for evil to occur is disconcerting because it suggests that horrors like genocide require involvement from large swaths of society, not simply social anomalies living in the margins. Indeed, according to

Arendt (1963/2006), "[t]he trouble with Eichmann was precisely that so many were like him, and that the many were neither perverted nor sadistic, that they were, and still are, terribly and terrifyingly normal" (p. 276). Banality is not a necessity for evil, but one is not precluded from being evil because they are banal (Barry, 2013). Those who contribute to evil in a banal way are arguably even more dangerous than Hitler. Although Hitler's passion for harming others seems like a rare trait, those resembling how Eichmann presented himself at his trial (despite arguably possessing moral flaws) are people whom we might encounter on a daily basis—even ourselves at times.

If we conceptualize Hitler as a villain who single-handedly perpetuated a horrific genocide, we can take some comfort in not having to consider how normal people like us were also part of the process. This false resolution of cognitive dissonance is dangerous when it prevents us from examining systemic factors, some of which are still in play today. Arendt's framework, however, provides a thoughtful platform for discussion as it explodes the binary of heroes and villains, leaving instead a sense of our own capabilities to lie somewhere on a continuum. Those who perpetuate evil are not extraordinary villains acting alone; rather, ordinary humans with ordinary lives perpetuating systemic harm, perhaps even with little to no consideration for how they might be contributing to evil. An explicit awareness of banal, extensive evil in social studies curriculum and pedagogy, in direct contrast with villainification, can help return thinking to these processes and restore a sense of personal agency.

Anti-villainification in Practice

Through an examination of both individual and systemic factors in a variety of spheres, students (and their teachers) are better able to see themselves within troubling situations, which then can lead to taking *action* instead of slipping into thoughtlessness as new social situations arise. This promotion of *action*, then, becomes an educational pursuit, rather than merely a topic of schooling. There are countless ways to usher in such student engagement. For example, teachers can explore this idea by: providing examples of banal evil, troubling the agency of supervillains, engaging with ethical entanglements, and paying attention to language and phrasing.

Specific Examples of Banal Evil

One method of anti-villainification education would be to pick an example of banal evil from a topic in the curriculum to flesh out with the students; for example, when teaching about the Second World War, reading an excerpt from Browning's (1993) book, *Ordinary Men*, such as:

> The deportation of largely unsuspecting Viennese Jews, most of them elderly and/or female, passed with so little incident that Lieutenant Fischmann could concentrate on the hardships of a third- rather than second-class car, insufficient rations, and the summer heat that spoiled his butter. No mention, of course, was made of what the incarcerated Jews, without food or water, must have been suffering in the closed cattle cars during the sixty-one hour journey. But Fischmann was quite conscious, as he delivered 949 Jews to the alleged work camp in Sobibór the gas chambers were deep in the forest and not visible from the unloading ramp. But contrary to most Order Police denials, Fischmann and his commando apparently entered the camp and watched the unloading. (p. 30)

What makes an excerpt like this powerful is that it: specifically names an otherwise unknown person, clearly explains his particular role in the atrocity, and reveals the accompanying thoughtlessness of his role. Such a description could then facilitate a discussion that illustrates how any human being can become an active participant in evil deeds, regardless of whether they intended to inflict harm.

It is vital to examine the underlying social context and systemic nature of large-scale harm, looking to its everyday nature, to groups and interconnected ordinary folks instead of a single hyperindividual. In the context of racially motivated violence, Goldsby (2006) illuminated the "cultural logic" of lynching to highlight the "networked, systemic phenomenon indicative of trends in national culture" (p. 5), thus revealing how ordinary people and processes contributed to the horrors of lynching in that "historical millieu" (p. 7). Key to this engagement is refraining from discounting all individual responsibility.

Lang (1990) noted a disturbing issue when teaching the Holocaust, namely that students can assume that Nazi soldiers were simply following orders, and, even if they were willing participants, they were merely a product of their education and background. Teachers cannot possibly tell all the stories of those involved in a historical situation, and yet it

48   C. van KESSEL

is important to avoid essentializing those groups. Avoiding harmful simplicity is, in part, how these groups are framed; for example, Gregory (2000) noted "the inadequacy of talk of *the* Jewish response" to the Nazis (p. 54). Instead, teachers might better talk of one response of many, carefully avoiding generalizations of thought and deeds of the larger collective.

Part of the purpose of understanding the historical milieu is to further extrapolate these processes into our present (or future) contexts. Timberg and Weisenberger (2013) mentioned a student who, after reading about Nazi ideology, remarked in his reading journal that: "It shows that Nazis were men, just as we are now. Desperate times try us all, and we must maintain our humanity and compassion for all, lest we end up justifying acts of barbarism in defense of nonsense ideology" (p. 54). Another student took the same reading to entail that people had to have been "brainwashed" by Hitler (p. 54). Although certainly this account shows an attempt by an educator to engage students with the idea of ordinary people in dark times, students can nonetheless separate themselves from those historical actors by issuing vague platitudes or by assuming a sort of non-thinking, instead of seeing the sort of thoughtlessness that can accompany otherwise moral, thinking humans like themselves. It is all too easy to say that "desperate times try us all," and yet fail to recognize similarly desperate times emerging in our contemporary lives.

Troubling the Singular Agency of Supervillains

A related task is to shift the focus away from a single villain and towards interconnected people and factors. This recognition highlights the importance of questioning the prevalent "morals" of a society when harm is being inflicted, such as racism and misogyny. Villainification can be observed with what might be called "regular" villains or "supervillains." An example of a supervillain would be Hitler, someone who is depicted and understood as more monster than human. A "regular" villain would be someone like Duncan Campbell Scott or Richard H. Pratt, both of whom have become figureheads for the extensive evil of residential schools.

The abuses of Indian Residential Schools in Canada and the United States are often understood through the deeds of individuals like the aforementioned Duncan Campbell Scott, who wrote about his intention "to get rid of the Indian problem" in 1920 (Leslie, 1978, p. 114). Yet, these deeds are more helpfully discussed as a nexus of individual and systemic factors that continue to perpetuate ideologies. The Truth and Reconciliation Commission of Canada (TRC, 2015) heard testimony from over six thousand survivors. Although some generalizations can certainly be made about how school administrators and teachers treated Indigenous peoples, individual experiences varied. In the U.S. context, similar simplifications around "Indian" education occur, where knowledge of the deculturalization (Spring, 2000) of Indigenous peoples often begins and ends with Captain Richard H. Pratt's (1892) plan to "kill the Indian and save the man." For some of those involved in residential schools, there might have been "good" intentions based upon religion, but these intentions were paired with a systemic thoughtlessness about how others were being harmed (e.g., a missionary mentality). However, there were also individuals who were overtly cruel (e.g., those who abused children).

How might we hold individuals accountable for their deeds while also recognizing the systemic, collective element beyond intentions, whether good or evil? Could we perhaps think of members in a society as guilty of thoughtlessness? Furthermore, how might we see the victims as more than passive recipients of evil deeds? The TRC (2015) encouraged survivors to tell not only their stories of suffering, but also their stories of resilience, and clearly demonstrates an appreciation for the individual, but interconnected, experiences of both victims and victimizers linked to their particular situations, contextualized within the historical milieu.

Although Duncan Campbell Scott or Richard H. Pratt may not be household names around the world as Hitler is, when many of us ponder the horrors that plagued the Indian Residential Schools, we might understand it through these individuals. "We" are certainly not like Hitler, but neither are we like Campbell Scott or Pratt. We can be left with the impression that the individual moral failings of these men led to their evil deeds, thus spawning numerous speculative science fiction plot lines about what might happen were such individuals assassinated. Social studies texts can contribute to this myopic view regarding the autonomy of historical and contemporary actors. A textbook analysis by Brown and Brown (2010) demonstrated how U.S. history textbooks portray racial violence as a series of aberrant, unrelated events or, in their words, "bad men doing bad things" (p. 60). Brown and Brown (2010) critiqued these curricular representations of racial violence because they fail to draw connections between individual actions and the structural arrangements that made those actions possible. Anti-villainification work extends Brown and Brown (2010) with the recognition that portrayals like "bad men doing bad things" remove the concept of evil—conceptualized as incidents of racial violence—from the daily lives of ordinary people, thus allowing for a dismissal of the possibility that one contributes to evil because evildoers are conceptualized as exceptional and thus unusual.

Ethical Entanglements

There has been recognition of ethical judgement or dimension in historical thinking, both in terms of how we assess the deeds of the past and how those deeds impact us today, thus making the study of history particularly meaningful for students and promoting active citizenship (e.g., Barton & Levstik, 2004; Seixas, 1993; Seixas & Morton, 2013). This element of historical thinking is a difficult task, however, given that educators are often unaware of the implicit ethical judgements in their own teaching and the materials in support of that teaching (Gibson, 2014). When teachers and students discuss Christopher Columbus, Kim Jong-Il, Osama bin Laden, Saddam Hussein, Pol Pot, and, of course, Adolf Hitler, ethical judgements abound, and yet are often left unexamined. It is not that ethics cannot come into play during these discussions; rather that we seek to prevent ethical judgements that hinder critical analyses (e.g., Hitler was morally flawed, thus the Holocaust happened, and thus further analysis rendered unnecessary).

The invocation of the evil villain dominates over nuanced discussions of structural factors resulting from a variety of attitudes and deeds. This recognition of complexity does not absolve people like Hitler of blame; it merely calls for an examination of context that may be reflective of similar processes currently at play in our own lives. Villains of historical and contemporary events are (in some cases, perhaps aptly) labelled as evil, and yet an unwanted side effect is for this label to shut down students' critical thought and concern for one's shared community (Biesta & Lawy, 2006). A sense of otherworldly evil can delimit the agency of ordinary people and thus can be detrimental to the development of citizens working towards a less violent future (den Heyer & van Kessel, 2015). Furthermore, the more (in)famous the villain, the less like "us" (i.e., ordinary folk) they appear.

The discourse on historical figures does not have to limit itself to whether that figure is heroified or vilified. Arendt's notion of *action* and the banality of evil provide an analytical framework that can be compared with Sylvia Wynter's (1995) discussion of *subjective understanding*. Wynter (1995) embraced the untidy, but generative, interrelatedness and goals of humans as a species in both "ecosystemic" and "global social-systemic" contexts (p. 8). In other words, humans can examine multiple sides of a person, event, or issue, holding the tension in our mind that there is no "right" answer. We can ascertain and assess these multiple interests without slipping into unhelpful assumptions that nothing can be known. Wynter (1995) traced webs of context that shaped Columbus' deeds ranging from religion to economics to ideas of sacrifice, and beyond. She neither demonizes nor apologizes for Columbus, and yet recognizes the horrors he inflicted upon Indigenous peoples. For the purposes of this chapter, let us focus in on the strategy of how we might begin to break dichotomous (and thus simplistic) understandings of polarizing historical figures:

> Given that, it is these narratively instituted cosmogonies whose "stereotyped images" and unitary systems of meanings, together with the signaling systems that they encode, function to regulate in the culture-specific "good/evil" terms of each order's sociogenic principle or governing code.... The taking the "stereotyped images" of our present categorical models... as the point of departure for an inquiry into the narrative and rhetorical strategies... should provide an opening onto the gaining of such knowledge *outside* the limits of our present culture's self-conception. (Wynter, 1995, p. 48, emphasis original)

By first addressing stereotyped images and then adding meaningful complexity to those images, we set in motion a generative process towards a subjective understanding.

While Wynter (1995) engaged with a basic assumption of the interconnected human as a biological species, Arendt's focus was on the interconnected human in the sociopolitical sphere. Both Wynter and Arendt shared a call for an enhanced awareness of the complexities inherent in our human condition, but Arendt was more concerned with how we might recognize harmful processes, and so her focus on the judgements after the fact is with a view to how our sense of agency and responsibility

52   C. van KESSEL

may be affected as new situations arise. Arendt (1968) was explicitly concerned with the genesis of the disorder, hunger, massacres, and injustices of the "dark times" she studied and lived:

> All this was real enough as it took place in public; there was nothing secret or mysterious about it. And still, it was by no means visible to all, nor was it at all easy to perceive it; for, until the very moment when catastrophe overtook everything and everybody, it was covered up not by realities but by the highly efficient talk and double-talk of nearly all official representatives who, without interruption and in many ingenious variations, explained away unpleasant facts and justified concerns. When we think of dark times and of people living and moving in them, we have to take this camouflage, emanating from and spread by "the establishment"—or, "the system," as it was then called—also into account. (Arendt, 1968, p. viii)

Individuals must take responsibility for their deeds, but it is unwise to place all the blame on a single person. Conversely, only blaming a vague entity like "society" is equally unproductive because that blame is too depersonalized. If we want to foster the hope that any of us can subvert harmful processes, we need to teach in between those two positions instead of examining history as an either/or situation between individuals and the collective. It is not that we, as members of a society, discard ethics; rather, we are called upon to engage in the entanglement of ethical situations, as opposed to simplifying ethics by only ascribing it to a leader. As Arendt (1968) has noted, it is difficult to see such processes as they are occurring. Perhaps this is an obvious statement, such as the cliché that "hindsight is 20/20." Regardless, the issue of our potential thoughtlessness during dark times is one that demands attention in social studies education and beyond.

Attention to Language and Phrasing

Timothy Stanley (1999) has already reminded us to be attentive to how we frame content like the atrocities of the Nazis, such as thinking deeply about numerous aspects, from using a past or present tense for verbs to the impossibility of an analogy. Rethinking horrific historical and contemporary events with Arendtian complexity requires attention to the language used to describe those perpetuating the situation; for example, by avoiding the label of evil, or, if employing the term, taking the time to discuss its power to shut down thinking with the class. In the context of Nazi Germany, a teacher might ask students if they would label Hitler as evil, what that might mean to them, and whether that prevents them from seeing him as a human they might encounter in their daily lives. Attention ought also to be paid to the subject in sentences; for example, is Hitler standing in for what was perpetuated also by other Nazis? Are the Nazis (or Germans, for that matter) standing in for what people from other countries are also culpable (e.g., anti-Semitism)? Furthermore, there would need to be direct discussions about the societal forces exacerbated by the Nazis; for example, illustrating how insidious racism is through discussing the Smithsonian exhibit of anti-Semitic propaganda aimed at children (Wecker, 2016).

A textbook created for the Advanced Placement European History course by McKay et al. (2011) has provided meaningful complexity to Nazism because of its attention to language and phrasing, though likely not enough to the figure of Hitler himself. Unfortunately, the authors predominantly name Hitler and/or the Nazi party as a whole, at times using "Nazi Germany" or simply "Germany" as the agent of action instead of those in the Nazi government, or further indicators of more specific human agency (van Kessel & Plots, in press). There is a brief biography of Hitler, although it merely notes his parentage and that he was a "mediocre" high school dropout (McKay et al., 2011, p. 901). The authors lack the necessary complexity to flesh out Hitler as a human being. Notable anti-villainification, however, occurs in other contexts. McKay et al. (2011) aptly pointed out that "Hitler was not alone" in his racism (p. 901) as "Nazi gangs" wreaked havoc during Kristallnacht (p. 904), while "[n]ot all Germans supported Hitler… and a number of German groups actively resisted him" (p. 907). The authors mentioned the roles of military commanders, policemen, bureaucrats, and other administrators, in addition to the Nazi armies, the Einsatzgruppen, and the Schutzstaffel (SS). In a crowning moment of anti-villainification, McKay et al. (2011) identified anti-Semitism, peer pressure, social advancement, Nazi propaganda, and other motivations as encouraging "ordinary Germans" to "join the SS ideologues and perpetuate ever-greater crimes, from mistreatment to arrest to mass murder" (pp. 913–914). The blame for the atrocities of the war is spread out among Germans, without diluting that blame. The authors even noted the role that the anti-Semitism of Europeans in general played, although

54   C. van KESSEL

notably without implicating the people of either Britain or the United States. The nuanced descriptions in this textbook potentially enrich students' understandings of the complexities that led to the horrors of the Second World War; however, Hitler himself still largely remains an oversimplified villain. There is a need to depict Hitler himself (and those who have played a similar role in history) with the level of complexity and detail that McKay et al. (2011) provided for the general German population.

Teaching Disobedience

Blind obedience has been revealed again and again as an incredibly harmful situation. Although it might be tempting to ascribe obedience to either a personality trait or a particular situation, psychological studies show that both are in play (Blass, 1991). Obedience is learned, but the process is complex: "different individuals are motivated in different degrees to be more or less obedient because of a complex socialization mix of learning to live up to expectations and of learning to trust and/or fear authority" (Hamachek, 1976, p. 445). Students need to learn that those in power (e.g., governments) are "not always ethical or moral" (Marks, 2017, p. 131) and can enact (and have enacted) perfectly legal but horrific deeds. The study of these instances (e.g., in Nazi Germany or during the Rwandan genocide) can be paired with the discussions of personal tendencies towards *authoritarian submission*, defined as a "submissive, uncritical attitude toward idealized moral authorities of the ingroup" (Adorno, Frenkel-Brunswik, Levinson, & Sanford, 1950, p. 228). The hope here is that educators will encourage the sort of critical thinking that is independent of authority. As we know from Milgram's (1965) work, the presence of others who show disobedience heightens our capabilities to stand up for what we know is right.

In terms of curriculum, we need to address the issue of obedience. Some students may assume that, for example, Nazi soldiers were simply following orders and, if willing participants, they were merely products of their education and background—there is little room for individual responsibility (Lang, 1990). Saltzman (2000) has taught a course on the psychology of the Holocaust, where personal and social factors are considered regarding those who participated in genocide. After beginning with historical context, the class considers "dispositional explanations for perpetrator behavior" that include Milgram's work, as well as psychiatric research on the Nuremberg war crimes defendants

(Borofsky & Brand, 1980; Zilmer, Harrower, Ritzler, & Archer, 1995) and Adorno et al. (1950) work on the authoritarian personality, among other works.

We also need to be careful to avoid unintentionally teaching blind obedience through our daily classroom activities. Gordon (1999) discussed the banality of evil in terms of day-to-day pedagogy. He calls for educators to avoid indicators of thoughtlessness in their teaching practice such as using "clichés and stock phrases" as responses to student input, encouraging students' "blind devotion and admiration" to the teacher, and creating climates of "falsehood and self- deception" (Gordon, 1999, pp. 26–28). We can encourage reasonable, not unconditional, obedience. Drawing from Hamachek (1976), there are many interrelated strategies, including teachers providing opportunities for students to: disagree with any intimidation or penalty, see authority figures as capable of mistakes, discuss reasons for rules and regulations, and explore examples of when it is acceptable or even desirable to be disobedient. Although it is important to study those who have been disobedient to authority in the past, it is equally important to discuss contemporary examples and to engage with disobedience directly in our classrooms.

IMPLICATIONS OF ANTI-VILLAINIFICATION

There is a tension between blaming one person for systemic, large-scale harm and diffusing blame into an amorphous entity (e.g., "society"). A singular focal point can prevent us from seeing our own responsibility, just as blaming society as a whole can be too impersonal to implicate ourselves. We are, thus, left with the question: How might we think, live, and educate in the tension between those two poles—a villain or a faceless mob? If we are to accept personal responsibility without shouldering the blame for what is also a product of "the system," then it behoves us to consider how we might talk about systemic harm. Ordinary people, living their mundane lives, can easily slip into the sort of thoughtlessness that Arendt (1963/2006) describes, with a cumulative effect of creating and sustaining systemic harm (in this case, irrevocable damage to the environment as well as the species with whom we share this planet). This thoughtlessness does not mean that any singular person— you, me, or anyone else—is to blame, rather, we ought to live in the tension between being neither innocent nor guilty. We can be genuinely thoughtful, examining our (in)actions and change as we realize that what we do (or do not do) matters. Instead of resolving our anxieties and fears by shifting blame onto a villain, we can consider how we might make changes that affect, and are amplified by, our interconnections.

It is dangerous to create villains in both historical and contemporary times. A focus on an individual at the expense of the whole allows us to shut down our thinking about the part that we all play, or could have played, in the atrocities we are quick to condemn and blame on a select few. That way, we avoid feelings of guilt. Yet, if we can shift from feelings of *guilt* to feelings of *responsibility*, perhaps we might be able to examine extensive evils with more nuance. Investigating the form and function of villainification can reinvigorate the complexity inherent in our human situation, pushing back against the ways school texts can portray historical actors, in which, "not only victims, but also victimizers, collaborators, resisters, bystanders, and rescuers were all individualized or collectively represented, normalized or exoticized, personalized or abstracted— that is, if their roles were included in the first place" (Schweber, 2004, p. 157). I specifically critique representations of the victimizers, who have undergone a process of villainification that propagates a form of thoughtlessness. Arendt's theory of evil implicates us all, serving as a call to take action in order to prevent further large-scale harm.

Resisting villainification thwarts historical and contemporary situations constructed as oversimplified conflicts between "good guys" and "bad guys." The complexity that ensues when villainification is avoided will "enable students and teachers to examine and erode dichotomies, such as us/them, inside/outside, individual/collective, here/there, and private/public … [which are] often constructed, deconstructed, and reconstructed through emotional and affective forces" (Helmsing, 2014, p. 128). This erosion contributes to more effective teaching of social studies by encouraging students and teachers to engage meaningfully with difficult knowledge (Britzman, 1998). When we add complexity to social traumas in the curriculum, including discussion of our own implication, we help prevent reductionist understandings of evil that shut down analysis and debate.

Villainification is not the only process in play that blocks thoughtfulness when studying extensive evils of the past and present. The *politics of evil* is the employment of the term evil against an oversimplified group by politicians in their rhetoric. Such rhetoric (intentionally or not) can stifle democratic debate and exacerbate hate speech because groups are generalized and stigmatized. What makes villainification distinct from the politics of evil is its emphasis on the individual; for example, Osama Bin Laden serves as a villain, while the politics of evil involves Al Qaeda, Islamic State of Iraq and the Levant (ISIL), or even the entire population of Muslims as an amorphous and oversimplified group. The politics of evil is discussed in Chapter 5.

Historical and contemporary events and figures need to be understood outside of the dichotomous thinking engendered by heroification and villainification narratives. Students become robbed of their sense of agency and responsibility if they learn that positive social change occurs through the deeds of extraordinary individuals rather than broad, coordinated mobilization of ordinary people, and that evil occurs at the whim of a "madman" rather than through everyday actions that support injustice. Villainification makes it more difficult to recognize and evaluate systemic factors, particularly vis-à-vis how we all might contribute to extensive evils at times. Thus, anti-villainification analyses are needed for deconstructing the binary of heroes and villains. The realization that ordinary people are, in fact, agents of change is an important lesson. I claim that deconstructing villainification, paired with an acceptance of the banality of evil (Arendt, 1963/2006) and a call for *action* (Arendt, 1958/1998), provides a sense of agency and responsibility in social studies curriculum and pedagogy. Without laying blame per se, anti-villainification processes call for an individual responsibility that, despite being uncomfortable, is necessary to provide meaningful complexity to discussions of historical and contemporary harm.

REFERENCES

Adorno, T. W., Frenkel-Brunswik, E., Levinson, D. J., & Sanford, R. N. (1950). *The authoritarian personality.* New York, NY: Harper & Row.

Alridge, D. (2006). The limits of master narratives in history textbooks: An analysis of representations of Martin Luther King, Jr. *Teachers College Record, 108,* 662–686. https://doi.org/10.1111/j.1467-9620.2006.00664.x.

Arendt, H. (1966). *The origins of totalitarianism* (New ed.). New York, NY: Harcourt, Brace & World. (Original work published in 1951)

Arendt, H. (1968). *Men in dark times.* New York, NY: Harcourt, Brace & World.

Arendt, H. (1998). *The human condition* (2nd ed.). Chicago, IL: University of Chicago Press. (Original work published in 1958)

Arendt, H. (2006). *Eichmann in Jerusalem: A report on the banality of evil.* New York, NY: Penguin. (Original work published in 1963)

58 C. van KESSEL

Aristotle. (1995). *Poetics* (S. Halliwell, Trans.). Cambridge, MA: Harvard University Press. (Original work published c. 335 B.C.E.)

Barry, P. B. (2013). *Evil and moral psychology.* New York, NY: Routledge.

Barton, K., & Levstik, L. (2004). *Teaching history for the common good.* Mahwah, NJ: Lawrence Erlbaum.

Bernstein, R. J. (2002). Reflections on radical evil: Arendt and Kant. *Soundings: An Interdisciplinary Journal, 85*(1/2), 17–30.

Bernstein, R. J. (2005). *The abuse of evil: The corruption of politics and religion since 9/11.* Malden, MA: Polity.

Biesta, G., & Lawy, R. (2006). From teaching citizenship to learning democracy: Overcoming individualism in research, policy and practice. *Cambridge Journal of Education, 36,* 63–79. https://doi.org/10.1080/03057640500490981.

Blass, T. (1991). Understanding behavior in the Milgram obedience experiment: The role of personality, situations, and their interactions. *Journal of Personality and Social Psychology, 60,* 398–413. https://doi.org/10.1037/0022-3514.60.3.398.

Borofsky, G. L., & Brand, D. J. (1980). Personality organization and psychological functioning of the Nuremberg war criminals: The Rorschach data. In J. Dimsdale (Ed.), *Survivors, victims and perpetrators: Essays on the Nazi Holocaust* (pp. 359–403). New York, NY: Hemisphere.

Britzman, D. P. (1998). *Lost subjects, contested objects: Toward a psychoanalytic inquiry of learning.* Albany: State University of New York Press.

Brown, A. L., & Brown, K. D. (2010). Strange fruit indeed: Interrogating contemporary textbook representations of racial violence toward African Americans. *Teachers College Record, 112,* 31–67.

Browning, C. R. (1993). *Ordinary men: Reserve Police Battalion 101 and the final solution in Poland.* New York, NY: Harper Perennial.

Browning, C. R. (2003). *Collected memories: Holocaust history and postwar testimony.* Madison: University of Wisconsin Press.

Coates, T.-N. (2013). The good, racist people. *The New York Times.* Retrieved from http://www.nytimes.com/2013/03/07/opinion/coates-the-good-racist-people.html.

den Heyer, K., & van Kessel, C. (2015). Evil, agency, and citizenship education. *McGill Journal of Education, 50*(1), 1–18.

Elon, A. (2006). Introduction. In H. Arendt, *Eichmann in Jerusalem: A report on the banality of evil* (pp. vii–xxiii). New York, NY: Penguin.

Epstein, T. L. (1994). Tales from two textbooks: A comparison of the civil rights movement in two secondary history textbooks. *The Social Studies, 85*(3), 121–126. https://doi.org/10.1080/00377996.1994.9956289.

3 BANAL EVIL AND SOCIAL STUDIES EDUCATION 59

Gibson, L. (2014). *Understanding ethical judgments in secondary school history classes* (Doctoral dissertation). Retrieved from http://hdl.handle.net/2429/48498.

Goldsby, J. (2006). *A spectacular secret: Lynching in American life and literature.* Chicago, IL: University of Chicago Press.

Gordon, M. (1999). Arendt and Conrad on the banality of evil: Some implications for education. *Journal of Thought, 34*(2), 15–30. Retrieved from http://www.jstor.org/stable/42589573.

Gregory, I. (2000). Teaching about the Holocaust: Perplexities, issues and suggestions. In I. Davies (Ed.), *Teaching the Holocaust: Educational dimensions, principles and practice* (pp. 49–60). London, UK: Continuum.

Hamachek, D. E. (1976). Removing the stigma from obedience behavior. *Phi Delta Kappan, 57,* 443–446. Retrieved from https://www.jstor.org/stable/20298318.

Harrington, A. (1969). *The immortalist.* Millbrae, CA: Celestial Arts.

Hatzfeld, J. (2006). *Machete season: The killers in Rwanda speak* (L. Coverdale, Trans.). New York, NY: Farrar, Straus and Giroux. (Original work published in 2003)

Helmsing, M. (2014). Virtuous subjects: A critical analysis of the affective substance of social studies education. *Theory & Research in Social Education, 42,* 127–140. https://doi.org/10.1080/00933104.2013.842530.

Kant, I. (1838). *Religion within the boundary of pure reason* (J. W. Semple, Trans.). Edinburgh, Scotland: Thomas Clark. (Original work published in 1793)

Kohl, H. (1991). The politics of children's literature: The story of Rosa Parks and the Montgomery bus boycott. *Journal of Education, 173,* 35–50.

Lang, B. (1990). *Act and idea in the Nazi genocide.* Chicago, IL: University of Chicago Press.

Leslie, J. (1978). *The historical development of the Indian Act* (2nd ed.). Ottawa, Canada: Department of Indian Affairs.

Liddell, H. G., & Scott, R. (1996). *A Greek-English lexicon.* Oxford, UK: Clarendon Press.

Loewen, J. W. (2007). *Lies my teacher told me: Everything your American history textbook got wrong.* New York, NY: Simon & Schuster.

Löfström, J. (2013). How Finnish upper secondary students conceive transgenerational responsibility and historical reparations: Implications for the history curriculum. *Journal of Curriculum Studies, 46,* 515–539. https://doi.org/10.1080/00220272.2013.859301.

Mann, L. (1973). Attitudes toward My Lai and obedience to orders: An Australian survey. *Australian Journal of Psychology, 25,* 11–21. https://doi.org/10.1080/00049537308255828.

Marks, M. J. (2017). Teaching the Holocaust as cautionary tale. *The Social Studies, 108,* 129. https://doi.org/10.1080/00377996.2017.1343790.

Matt. (2013, December 23). *The Milgram experiment (full film)* [Video file]. Retrieved from https://www.youtube.com/watch?v=wdUu3u9Web4.

McKay, J. P., Hill, B. D., Buckler, J., Crowston, C. H., Wiesner-Hanks, M. E., & Perry, J. (2011). *A history of Western society since 1300 for advanced placement* (10th ed.). Boston, MA: Bedford/St. Martin's.

Milgram, S. (1963). Behavioral study of obedience. *Journal of Abnormal and Social Psychology, 67,* 371–378.

Milgram, S. (1965). Liberating effects of group pressure. *Journal of Personality and Social Psychology, 1,* 127–134.

Minnich, E. (2014). The evil of banality: Arendt revisited. *Arts & Humanities in Higher Education, 13,* 158–179. https://doi.org/10.1177/1474022213513543.

Novick, P. (1999). *The Holocaust in American life.* New York, NY: Houghton Mifflin.

Pratt, R. (1892). Kill the Indian, save the man. *Official report of the nineteenth annual conference of charity and correction,* 46–59.

Saltzman, A. L. (2000). The role of obedience experiments in Holocaust studies: The case for renewed visibility. In T. Blass (Ed.), *Obedience to authority: Current perspectives on the Milgram paradigm* (pp. 125–144). Mahwah, NJ: Lawrence Erlbaum.

Schweber, S. A. (2004). *Making sense of the Holocaust: Lessons from classroom practice.* New York, NY: Teachers College Press.

Seixas, P. (1993). Historical understanding among adolescents in a multicultural setting. *Curriculum Inquiry, 23,* 301–327.

Seixas, P., & Morton, T. (2013). *The big six: Historical thinking concepts.* Toronto, Canada: Nelson Education.

Selman, R. L., & Barr, D. B. (2009). Can adolescents learn to create ethical relationships for themselves in the future by reflecting on ethical violations faced by others in the past? In M. Martens, U. Hartmann, M. Sauer, & M. Hasselhorn (Eds.), *Interpersonal understanding in historical context* (pp. 19–41). Rotterdam, The Netherlands: Sense.

Spring, J. (2000). *Deculturalization and the struggle for equality: A brief history of the education of dominated cultures in the United States.* New York, NY: Routledge.

Stangneth, B. (2015). *Eichmann before Jerusalem: The unexamined life of a mass murderer.* New York, NY: Penguin Random House.

Stanley, T. (1999). A letter to my children: Historical memory and the silences of childhood. In J. P. Robertson (Ed.), *Teaching for a tolerant world, grades K-6: Essays and resources* (pp. 34–44). Urbana, IL: National Council for Teachers of English.

Timberg, H., & Weisberger, R. (2013). *Teaching, learning, and the Holocaust: An integrative approach.* Bloomington: Indiana University Press.

Truth and Reconciliation Commission of Canada. (2015). *Honouring the truth, reconciling for the future: Summary of the final report of the Truth and Conciliation Commission of Canada.* Retrieved from http://www.trc.ca/websites/trcinstitution/File/2015/Honouring_the_Truth_Reconciling_for_the_Future_July_23_2015.pdf.

van Kessel, C. (2018). Banal and fetishized evil: Implicating ordinary folk in genocide education. *Journal of International Social Studies, 8*(2), 160–171. Retrieved from http://www.iajiss.org/index.php/iajiss/article/view/377.

van Kessel, C., & Crowley, R. M. (2017). Villainification and evil in social studies education. *Theory & Research in Social Education, 95*(4), 427–455. https://doi.org/10.1080/00933104.2017.1285734.

van Kessel, C., & Plots, R. (in press). A textbook study in villainification: The need to renovate our depictions of villains. *One World in Dialogue.*

Waller, J. (2007). *Becoming evil: How ordinary people commit genocide and mass killing* (2nd ed.). Oxford, UK: Oxford University Press.

Wecker, M. (2016, June 27). How the Nazis "normalized" anti-Semitism by appealing to children: A new museum and exhibit explore the depths of hatred toward Europe's Jews. *Smithsonian.* Retrieved from http://www.smithsonianmag.com/history/how-nazi-normalized-anti-semitism-appealing-children-180959539/.

Woodson, A. N. (2016). We're just ordinary people: Messianic master narratives and black youths' civic agency. *Theory & Research in Social Education, 44,* 184–211. https://doi.org/10.1080/00933104.2016.1170645.

Wynter, S. (1995). 1492: A new world view. In V. Lawrence Hyatt & R. Nettleford (Eds.), *Race, discourse, and the origin of the Americas: A new world view* (pp. 5–57). Washington, DC: Smithsonian Institution Press.

Zilmer, E. A., Harrower, M., Ritzler, B. A., & Archer, R. P. (1995). *The quest for the Nazi personality: A psychological investigation of Nazi war criminals.* The LEA series in personality and clinical psychology. Hillsdale, NJ: Lawrence Erlbaum.

CHAPTER 4

Processes of Evil as a Supplement to Citizenship Education

What makes a good citizen? What are educators trying to accomplish with "citizenship" education? This chapter engages with a supplement to citizenship education through Alain Badiou's identification of three processes of evil: betrayal, simulacrum/terror, and disaster. According to Badiou (1993/2001), evil is not something that exists on its own; rather, evil is a failure of the good. He defined evil as the result of humans failing or perverting a *truth procedure* (i.e., the activity of an emerging truth). We need a set of ethics to help create a world with less evil—to persevere in our goodness—despite the established order of things that might discourage us.

ALAIN BADIOU

Alain Badiou, born in 1937, is a French philosopher concerned with the concepts of being and truth. He has taught at the lycée in Reims, the Université of Paris VIII, the École normale supérieure (Paris), among other institutions. Likely influenced by his mathematician father, Badiou develops his ideas about truth procedures through Set Theory, drawing upon the disciplined openness from the field. Considered to be an Althusserian structural Marxist, Badiou was influenced by the student uprisings of May 1968 and perhaps also by his father's role in the French Resistance during the Second World War. Badiou, however, is not limited to Althusser and Marx and has engaged with other thinkers

© The Author(s) 2019

C. van Kessel, *An Education in 'Evil'*,
Palgrave Studies in Educational Futures,
https://doi.org/10.1007/978-3-030-16605-2_4

63

64   C. van KESSEL

such as Baruch Spinoza. Badiou seeks ways to develop the intellectual and resources to make emancipatory, egalitarian changes to our world (Hallward, 2013).

CONTEXTS FOR CITIZENSHIP EDUCATION

Often civic education is housed in subject areas such as government, history, and social studies education. Informally, civics can haunt other subject areas, as well as the general functioning of schools (e.g., mission statements). In the context of the United States, Canada, and elsewhere, an accepted definition of a citizen is "someone who belongs to a country and upholds its political institution" (Schmidt, 2010, p. 109). This definition entails a need to understand the history and functioning of political institutions and the citizen's potential places within those institutions. Parker (2003) considered a strong form of democratic citizenship education to include "nurturing the kind of democratic political community that in turn protects and nurtures cultural pluralism and equality, which in turn protect and nurture a democratic political community" (p. xvii), and thus requires independent judgement about what might be just or unjust in a particular context, and the courage to take action accordingly.

Some education scholars expand civic education into global citizenship education, and yet this framing cannot only fail to thwart petty nationalism, but also reify the nation as "a unique social, political, cultural entity that deserves special attention and is fundamentally unlike the rest of the world" (Gaudelli, 2003, p. 126). During the twentieth century in Canada, for example, global citizenship was developed as a source of pride for Canada as a nation (Richardson, 2002), as a member of the British Empire and the Commonwealth (Willinsky, 1998) and also as a player on the global stage as a peacekeeping presence and/or environmental leader (e.g., Byers, 2012). In this way, a global framing can ironically narrow the focus down to the nation, as Canadians can (somewhat ironically) haughtily assert their global (supposed) "niceness" particularly in contrast with their counterparts in the United States.

Critical theorists have added to citizenship education a sense of questioning and a drive for equality. Who is privileged and who is marginalized? How might we engage these systems differently? As such, democracy is "a process that requires deliberation, not a product" (Schmidt, 2010, p. 109). For example, citizens can be thought of as participatory, personally responsible, and/or social justice oriented (Westheimer & Kahne, 2004). These categories delineate between the extent of active participation. Personally responsible citizens take part in institutions and events, such as donating to a food drive. Participatory citizens take the initiative, such as identifying the need for a food drive and organizing it. Justice-oriented citizens ask the tough questions; they deliberate on the functioning of society. Citizens who are justice oriented are the ones who question why some are going hungry while others have more food than they need. These critical stances raise key questions about existing structures and identify injustices that ought to be remedied.

In addition to critical perspectives, I feel that we need also offer provocations about citizenship as an affirmative stance. The task then becomes less about educating specifically good "citizens" and more about education that is connected "to love for the world" (Hodgson, Vlieghe, & Zamojski, 2017, p. 19). In this way, we might take up a particular sense of cosmopolitanism, but one that is not cultural or nationalistic—and thus potentially destructive (Pinar, 2011; Spector, 2017). Cosmopolitanism can be less imposed and anthropocentric, engaging with the ineradicable links to "not only all other earthly creatures but to the entire ecosystem" (Spector, 2015, p. 425. See also Arendt, 1958/1998). In other words, the planet needs to be considered as much as the humans and other entities upon it. Although it remains important to learn concepts like political systems and our potential places within them, as well as to become socialized into a society's fabric, the more interesting task is to develop individuals who think independently from authority, but who are simultaneously interconnected with other humans and entities with whom we share this planet. This task is separated from nationhood, but nonetheless connected to others—human and beyond—but without the limitations of a nation or state. In this way, Alain Badiou's processes of evil provide a platform to engage with such meaningful ponderings.

BADIOU'S GENERAL ANTHROPOLOGY OF TRUTHS

Before delving into Badiou's understanding of evil, we must first explore his idea of truths. This framing is fundamental to how Badiou sees the world. For many philosophers, theologians, and others, evil exists independently from what is good, and we must seek to eradicate it through a definable set of thoughts and actions (or inactions). Such an idea stems from the idea of a priori evil and thus "Good" is how we react to "Evil" (e.g., creating human rights to counteract crimes against humanity). According to Badiou (1993/2001), this understanding is flawed because it:

1. identifies a generic human subject and the evil that befalls them;
2. assumes that ethics will guide politics, with the spectator judging the circumstances accordingly; and
3. hypothesizes that Good derives from a reaction to Evil, rather than the opposite.

Attempts to prevent the repetition of the evils of the past have largely failed; for example, since the worldwide cry of "never again" in the mid-twentieth century, several genocides have been perpetuated: Bosnia, Rwanda, Darfur, and more. This realization can lead to a pessimistic belief that a violent future is inevitable and our only possibility. Students in my own classroom have expressed dismay at our lack of "progress," despite "advances" like the creation of the United Nations. According to Badiou, the problem lies in our understanding of ethics, not in the failure of human nature. Having an extremely negative example like the Holocaust has created a cycle that does a disservice not only to Jews but also to current and future victims of such violence. The horrific actions of the Nazis are deemed unique in history and yet are constantly referenced (in some arguably similar situations, like Bosnia, but also in even less similar situations). At any rate, this paradox of imitation of the inimitable not only prevents us from properly diagnosing what happened in Germany in the mid-twentieth century as "a political sequence," but it also prevents us from seeing "the creation of new singularities of Evil" (Badiou, 1993/2001, pp. 64–65). Furthermore, conceptualizing humans as purely as victims ignore our political context such as the contempt shown by so-called civilizing forces towards the situation including the victims themselves. Badiou draws a poignant comparison between France and Nazism. Both Vichy France and modern France have defined Others (first Jews and now illegal immigrants) according to an ethics of economic "necessity" (Badiou, 1993/2001, p. 33), and this ethic perpetuates evil actions. To truly move forward, we must tear ourselves away from nihilism and despair by basing ethics upon affirming truths against the desire for nothingness

(Badiou, 1993/2001, p. 39). The unthought that characterizes our contemporary sense of ethics can be replaced by thoughtfulness and fidelity to a truth. Thus, false ideas/ideals of necessity and nihilism can give way to a new way of being. The existence of truths, rather than the evil of trying to implement one single Truth, opens up individuals and society to infinite possibilities.

Badiou understands the situation in an opposite fashion than what is common philosophically and otherwise: Evil only exists in relation to what might be Good. Evil is not its own entity, drive, or propensity; it is a process. Evil exists as a dimension of truth procedures, not simply a rejection or neglect of the Good, and such affirmative thought makes humans distinct from animals. This premise seeks to subvert conceptualizations that devaluing humans as entities, that:

> equat[e] man [sic] with his animal substructure... to be sure humanity is an animal species. It is mortal and predatory. But neither of these attributes can distinguish humanity from within the world of the living. In his role as executioner, man is an animal abjection, but we must have the courage to add that in his role as victim, he is generally worth little more. (Badiou, 1993/2001, p. 11)

In other words, when we accept the horrors of the torturer and tortured as the result of an abstract Evil rather than a result of inadequate responses or perversions of the Good, we are dwelling unhelpfully in our own creatureliness.

Badiou begins with a premise of equality (although arguably anthropocentric). Every human being has equal capacities for "Good," but the *universal* is rooted in the *particular*. Although anyone can encounter an event at any time, without the prerequisite of any special qualities or knowledge, that event is relational to that person at a particular place and time. Differences in identities (e.g., ethnoracial, gender, political) or qualifications (e.g., level of schooling) do not bar us from encountering a truth. Differences exist and seem infinite: There "are as many differences, say, between a Chinese peasant and a young Norwegian professional as between myself and anybody at all, including myself" (Badiou, 1993/2001, p. 26). Divisions based on race, class, or any other differences have no bearing on truths, which are "indifferent to difference" (Badiou, 1993/2001, p. 27). It does not matter who or where you are, all of us have an equal capacity to encounter a truth procedure, and it is

68   C. van KESSEL

important to develop a set of ethics that upholds this sense of equality, so that a becoming subject is not barred from pursuing the truth they encounter.

The differences that so often divide us in both our daily lives (and on the world stage) ought not to: "since differences are what there is, and since every truth is the coming-to-be of that which is not yet, so differences then are precisely what truths depose, or render insignificant" (Badiou, 1993/2001, p. 27). Along this line of thinking, racism, sexism, ableism, and other prejudices cause harm not only for obvious reasons, but also because they deny this inherent equality in relation to truths. Differences do indeed affect our daily lives and at times can catastrophically block us from pursuing our truths. As such, we need to be careful not to shut down the lived experiences of those underserved by our present system that fetishizes difference, we must "ensure that [Badiou's] work is not used to diminish the voices, perspectives, or agency of those who bear the brunt of all the forms exclusion takes" (den Heyer, 2009, p. 463). It is vital that an educational (or any) engagement with Badiou's philosophy is not used to perpetuate existing divisions among humans.

Truth Procedures

A truth procedure is the process of engaging with a situation once the images and ideas we have learned about such situations have shattered. As we are "going about our business," we will be shocked by a moment when we realize that what we had assumed or taken for granted is incomplete, wrong, or otherwise in need of rethinking (e.g., when someone realizes that they have been privileged or oppressed by a system that they had previously been unaware of). A comparison here can be made to Dąbrowski's (1964) theory of positive disintegration, whereby certain constraints from socialization/integration need to be disintegrated for individual existential choices to occur (e.g., dissent from authority or the norm). Such a shattering (or disintegration) occurs when we come across what Badiou calls an *event*. The meaning of event varies greatly among philosophers. For Badiou, an event is an irreducible singularity which supplements our ordinary experiences—it is an encounter with the *void*. The void is a vanishing point that shatters the legitimacy of what we had thought or desired:

at any given and unpredictable moment one may encounter a person, a thought, a question, that causes an "event" utterly voiding the legitimacy of what we just had thought or desired about ourselves or anything in particular (e.g., how falling in love shatters everything we thought about 'our' situation as any-'one' minding our own business before the "event" of "falling" in love). (den Heyer, 2015, p. 14)

An encounter with the void is an opportunity to rethink all the points we took as the realities of our situation; that is, we question what we had taken for granted. Our concept of reality is ruptured, and thus we create space for new thinking. An "event" propels us from our ordinary situations of opinions, of simply "what there is [*ce qu'il y a*]" into a new state of being of a truth process (Badiou, 1993/2001, p. 41). Events supplement our ordinary circumstances, and these processes are transformative. Becoming subjects partake in a "trans-individual act" via an event—a subjective experience that ties people together in a way that is radical because "it does not originate in any structure supported within being or the situation, such as the socio-economic" (Critchley, 2012, p. 26). The void is "the multiple of nothing, [and thus] neither excludes nor constrains anyone" (Badiou, 2001, p. 73).

A person, thought, or really anything can instigate such an event; however, we cannot predict or manufacture an event. All we can do is be attentive to an event's possibility (den Heyer & Conrad, 2011). Furthermore, truths do not set a firm path for us to follow—Badiou does not offer a step-by-step guide to truth procedures. Unlike a law that must be followed, often in a very particular way, an event creates opportunity:

[An event] is merely a proposition... The event creates a possibility but there, then, has to be an effort – a group effort in the political context, an individual one in the case of artistic creation – for this possibility to become real... Events are the creation in the world of the possibility of a truth procedure and not that which create this procedure itself. (Badiou & Tarby, 2013, p. 10)

An event is both situated and supplementary, and is thus *relational*, but not in the postmodern sense of everything being *relative*. Instead of being arbitrary, there is a void per each situation that an event can name.

70   C. van KESSEL

Fidelity to Our Truth Procedures

When an event occurs (e.g., falling in love), we must remain faithful to it by thinking about the present situation from the perspective of the event as *becoming subjects* (Badiou, 1993/2001, pp. 41–42). We then have the opportunity "to invent a new way of being and acting in the situation" (p. 42). The event triggers a truth procedure, and we then are called upon to remain steadfastly faithful by: moving within this novel situation, thinking about it in relation to the event, and finally inventing this new way of being whether it be in love, art, science, or politics.

The uncontrollable nature of an event opens up potentialities that we did not previously realize, but, in turn, we must actively strive to honour our truth procedure:

> The event creates a possibility but there, then, has to be an effort—a group effort in the political context, an individual one in the case of artistic creation—for this possibility to become real. (Badiou & Tarby, 2010/2013, p. 10)

For Badiou, the only prescription is a call to be faithful to the truth procedure; it does not set a firm path for us to follow. In this sense, Badiou is not constructing a philosophical system, but rather "a general anthropology of truth" (Barbour, 2010, p. 253). Badiou does not prescribe a truth; instead, he lays the foundation for us to identify and follow any one of many truth procedures. You can then choose (or not) to pursue a truth procedure that results from an event and breaks through what you had previously considered to be common sense. Fidelity to a truth procedure is the essence of ethics.

THE THREE EVILS

Alain Badiou (1993/2001) posits that instead of trying to transcend Evil and embody Good, we might see ourselves as "*beneath* Good and Evil" in a much more disorganized fashion (Badiou, 1993/2001, p. 59, emphasis original). Evil is not a thing in itself, but stems from: (1) *betraying* your truth procedure; (2) mistaking *simulacra* for truth procedures; and (3) imposing your truth upon others, which he calls *disaster*. Evil, thus, does not exist as a distinct entity. Instead, "there can be Evil only in so far as there precedes a Good" (p. 71).

Betrayal

Betrayal is the most mundane of the evils Badiou identifies. It is a failure to follow a truth procedure for such ordinary reasons such as corruption, exhaustion, or social discouragement. For example, Haydn could have easily given up on classical music when he faced opposition from those loyal to the normative Baroque style, and Romeo and Juliet could have forsaken their love. Following a new path can be frightening to a becoming subject, and the effort required to maintain a new way of thinking is no easy task, especially when your truth procedure runs contrary to social norms.

In contrast with the evil of betrayal, becoming subjects are able to remain militant in their fidelity because they trust in the universality of the event they experienced. If people see only their own particularity, then the truth process will be subverted. Something exists (the truth procedure) that is larger than ourselves as individuals. In the case of love, we are not the individual that we had assumed that we were. We are intimately (figuratively, but obviously also often literally) connected to another-"One" and together there is an interconnected existence. When that love is in relation to a shattering in art, politics, or another situation, again there is an opportunity to expand from a hyper-individualized framing of our existence.

Simulacrum

Simulacrum, according to Badiou, is a sort of false truth procedure that occurs when a radical break in a situation convokes not the void but the "full" particularity or presumed substance of the situation with which we are dealing (Badiou, 1993/2001, p. 73). In other words, an event—a shattering—has not happened. The supposed novelty is, in fact, part of the situation already in existence and can refer to plentitude, fulfilment, or destiny (e.g., of a people) rather than the void at the heart of all situations. If we believe that we are on the path of truth but have not engaged in the void, then we are adhering to a simulacrum, not a truth.

A simulacrum only appears to be an event. What the individual names as the site of the event is only what superficially appears to be the site. Thus, the individual remains an individual and does not become a subject (Smith, 2006, p. 96). This pseudo-event stands in stark contrast with an encounter with the void. A true event is an opportunity to rethink what we had taken as the realities of our situation, whereas a simulacrum reinforces something already in existence for a select group of people, thus preventing new thinking. The pseudo-event, the simulacrum, "then become[s] *identified* with an already established group" (Smith, 2006, p. 96). These already established peoples, the pseudo-subjects, are the only ones addressed by the simulacrum, in contrast with an event that is open to any becoming subject.

As an example of the evil of simulacrum/terror, Badiou (1993/2001) discusses the German Nazis of 1932–1945. Instead of seeking a break with the contemporary situation and the production of a new truth, the Nazis invoked the same sort of petty nationalism with which history is rife. The Nazi pursuit of a supposed truth was nothing more than a "continuity with [that which came] before...faithful only to the alleged national substance of a people" (Badiou, 1993/2001, p. 73). The Nazis assumed one way to be German, one way to be a Jew, and so on. Becoming subjects could not be created because the Nazis had already preordained who were included (Aryans) and who were not (non-Aryans), and furthermore, these categories tapped into pre-existing notions of identity and politics. Thus, the Nazi "event" was a pseudo-event—a simulacrum.

Related to simulacrum of truths is Badiou's notion of *terror*. Those who challenge the adherence to a simulacrum are discarded as detrimental to the promised day-to-come. An example of terror would be the Jacobin Committee of Public Safety who guillotined not only those who were opposed to their version of the revolution but also those who were moderates. Those who fail to uphold the simulacrum face the wrath of the regime (e.g., the White Rose group of university students in Germany who were executed for defying the Nazis), and yet there are those who nonetheless resisted, such as the Danes who relayed intelligence, sabotaged the occupying Nazis, and rescued most Jews in Denmark from certain death (Burgan, 2010).

Some scholars of Badiou see issues with the identifying of something as simulacrum; for example, Taubman (2010) argued that one might see the U.S.-led war on Iraq after the events of 11 September 2001 equally as an event or a simulacrum (p. 202). In my interpretation of Badiou, I agree with Taubman that, given the details and duration of the invasion, it might be difficult to determine the status of that occurrence; however, I interpret the war on Iraq as *disaster*, the third and final of Badiou's evils, as the supposed quest for democracy was imposed as a single truth.

Disaster

I consider disaster to be the most obnoxious form of evil. Disaster consists of the imposition of a truth out of arrogance, attempting to make this truth objective and absolute, trying to make a single ("capital T") Truth universally applicable. Badiou (1993/2001) is very clear that truths (notably in the plural) are relational and personal, as he says: "truth is entirely subjective" (p. 14). Although truths indeed exist, they are unique to each becoming subject and thus cannot be imposed upon others.

The mythological figure of Procrustes is a helpful allegory. The ancient Greeks considered hospitality to be sacred, and Procrustes was the monster who violated that principle. Guests in his home were forced to fit the guest bed exactly. If they did not fit the length of the bed perfectly, Procrustes would resize them through torture: amputation if too tall or stretching if too short. His idea of perfection (or, for our purposes, "truth") was forced upon all of his ill-fated guests. Populations can be seriously harmed by a one-Truth-fits-all that confuses subjective truth with objective knowledge, regardless of whether the intentions are to help or harm. Charlemagne forced people to convert to Christianity or die at the sword, the Red Guards attacked intellectuals physically and psychologically during the Chinese Cultural Revolution, members of the U.S. government forced their vision of democracy in places like Iraq (among many others), and Canadian government officials forced Western culture on Indigenous populations by means of Residential Schools. Some arguably may have had good intentions, but, regardless, imposing a subjective truth upon others is a violent act—intellectually, emotionally, and physically.

Evil, then, is a perversion only possible as a potential result of truth procedures in the form of *betrayal*, simulacrum-*terror*, and *disaster*: "terror, betrayal, and disaster are what an ethic of truths... tries to ward off... And [it] is certain that there can be Evil only in so far as there precedes a Good" (Badiou, 1993/2001, p. 71). It is not a matter of resisting evil but preventing it. Persevering with a truth procedure despite hardships, while being mindful of the dangers of simulacra and disaster, could subvert the creation or continuation of evil.

Eventful Education

Key scholars have been engaging with Badiou's philosophy in education, and after outlining some of the good work there, I will examine the possibility of engaging with Badiou's sense of evil specifically as

74   C. van KESSEL

a supplement to citizenship education. For the sake of brevity, we will focus on how: A. J. Bartlett examined an education by the state in contrast with an education by truths, Charles Barbour focused on the politics of difference as related to democratic education, and Kent den Heyer has seen the possibilities for education as an affirmative invention.

Education by the State vs. by Truths

Bartlett (2006) exposed the rivalry between education by the state and an education by truths, an idea that he expanded upon in his later book, *Badiou and Plato: An Education by Truths* (2011). He presented a new reading of Plato in the light of Badiou's idea of education, which juxtaposed the common contemporary fascination with *state* schooling (i.e., training without wisdom or truth) and *opinions* (in Badiou's sense of the encyclopaedia—that opinions are conformist views about the current situation). With Badiou's six components of truth procedures as chapters (state, site, event, fidelity, subject, and the generic), Bartlett (2011) related Badiou's philosophy to Plato's, and by offering a conceptualization of non-state education, Bartlett (2011) affirmed the link between truth and education. Like the many scholars of Arendtian *action*, Bartlett (2011) provided a meaningful framework to rethink pedagogy. In this case, Bartlett (2011) called for an education based upon *wisdom* instead of *sophistry* (p. 3; den Heyer, 2014), sophistry being linked to techniques and information devoid of thoughtfulness and the potential for new learning. Bartlett (2011) engaged with Plato's critique of sophistry:

> Plato's criticism of sophistry turns on two related things; ignorance and conceit. What the sophist is ignorant of is that his belief or opinion (they are the same thing) is not knowledge. In this sense the sophist imitates in ignorance of the fact that he imitates. (Bartlett, 2011, p. 44)

I relate such ignorance to the banality of evil; thoughtlessness is an ever-present danger to society in general and education specifically. Hollow thinking is schooling/sophistry, not education. Sophistry involves reasoned arguments, even logic, but not truth—and especially not a truth procedure in Badiou's sense. There is no openness with sophistry, only a defined outcome. Thus, an inquiry-driven classroom open to truth procedures must be wary of sophistry, which is, in a sense, a form of banality of evil due to its lack of thinking in a public sense.

Politics of Difference and Democratic Education

The notion of equality is another valuable extension of Badiou in an educational context. Barbour (2010) engaged with Badiou and Rancière to challenge the politics of difference and encourage a democratic approach to education. In Barbour's reading of Rancière, he understood equality as "an equal capacity to generate a new distribution of the sensible" (p. 261) and is "the condition rather than the goal of genuinely democratic political statements" (p. 260). By distribution of the sensible, Barbour (2010) referred to Rancière's aesthetic regime, or form of organization, that determines the possibilities for what people can think and do. Democracy, then, occurs when there is a new distribution of the sensible. As Barbour (2010) stated: "[P]olitics involves a moment of 'dissensus', or an antagonism that is not containable within 'the opposition of interests and opinions'" (p. 260). In Badiou's terms, there is a political event, which similarly does not require anyone to have special status or characteristics. What is required is the sort of thinking that is independent from authority:

> Truth, then, is not the result of a laborious process of self-reflection, much less something that can be arrived at through the protocols of instruction or submission to a master. Instead, a truth-event is something that almost miraculously happens. (p. 253)

Truth cannot be imposed; it must emerge. How might we take this up in our system of education?

The theory of truth procedures from events can frame curricula in a way that supports meaningful social justice aims. It is easy to see difference as a problem to be resolved (e.g., "How might we get along *despite* our differences?"), and yet through Badiou's philosophy, difference is simply the normal state of affairs. Any of us can encounter truths at any time, and thus our quest becomes to maintain our fidelity to those we encounter. Although we cannot create an event, we can arrange knowledge/curriculum to, for example, encounter the nexus of privilege and ignorance, and then students and teachers might see their agency in, and responsibility for, the world (den Heyer & Conrad, 2011). Any human is capable of a truth procedure, just like anyone can fall in love. Thus, identity politics can shut down the possibilities for truth-events, such as the principles of inclusion and representation, both of which suggest that "all subject-positions

76 C. van KESSEL

are reducible to interests, or can be located within a grid of recognizable power-relations" (Barbour, 2010, p. 253). Instead, it is better suited to embark on an ethical journey to foster an environment of equality and insight, both of which are fundamental aspects of a just society.

Education as Affirmative Invention

Ethical journeys in education call for an "arrangement of knowledge," as explored in den Heyer's (2009) article on education as an affirmative invention. It behoves us to consider and debate how we might organize curricula and create "institutional space for truths to emerge from such creative and inventive potential" (den Heyer, 2009, p. 460). As such, den Heyer (2009) pointed to examining "probability reasoning about futures more desirable and those less so" as a site of educational potential (p. 460). It is all too easy to attempt to predict the future, without a close examination of *why* we deem one scenario more probable than other (i.e., how the situation might feel prescribed), and thus limits discussion over how things might be different. It is valuable to devote time to such considerations because new ideas, and thus new truth procedures, have the space to emerge.

Such environments sharply contrast the sorts of classrooms created by the process of "customerization" in the same vein as the service industry. Teachers, instructors, and professors are responsible for helping students obtain the grades and/or training with the main goal of earning income and status, but Badiou's philosophy can be a basis to think politically rather than simply managerially (Strahan, 2010). Through an analysis of the purposes of schooling and Badiou's idea of the event, den Heyer (2015) elaborated on possible ways to engage in *education* rather than more managerial aims like qualification and socialization.

EVIL EDUCATION AS LOVE FOR THE WORLD?

Bartlett, Barbour, and den Heyer have made a strong case for how education might encourage fidelity to truth procedures. These arguments alone constitute a meaningful alternative or supplement to what we might consider to be citizenship education, but we can add to these arguments a specific focus on Badiou's understandings of evil. My choice of the word "supplement" is intentional. Events supplement our normal existence, and I think there is an opportunity for this philosophy of evil to similarly provoke the sort of shattering that can become an event.

When we start with the premise that evil exists as its own entity, then we run the risk of (ironically) limiting our ability to decrease the amount of evil. The repetition and continuation of violence and cruelty throughout history can be disheartening. After all, we have rules and laws, like the *Universal Declaration of Human Rights*, which states: "no one shall be held in slavery or servitude; slavery and the slave trade shall be prohibited in all their forms" (Article 4). Yet, slavery continues to plague the world often under the euphemistic term "human trafficking" despite United Nations efforts:

> Every year, thousands of men, women and children fall into the hands of traffickers, in their own countries and abroad. Almost every country in the world is affected by trafficking, whether as a country of origin, transit or destination for victims. (United Nations Office on Drugs and Crime, 2013)

Punishing the actions of those perpetuating evil is inadequate on its own (although certainly necessary). Punishment happens subsequently, after much damage has already been done and the evil is often exacerbated by the lengthy process of recognizing and then prosecuting the ill deed. When teachers ask their students why the Second World War erupted, the expected answer is often one or more causes such as the invasion of Poland or the rise of ultranationalism. It is rare, however, that the root causes of why such a war (or any war, for that matter) could have occurred at all. By not considering how our approach to ethics and human nature affects our relations on small and large scales, it is no wonder that many people expect future international conflict to be resolved in a similar manner (violence) or not resolved at all. We need to engage students in envisaging other possibilities, and engaging them with intellectual tools to make those egalitarian and emancipatory changes—this process is a meaningful form of citizenship education.

According to Gert Biesta (2010), good education promotes active participation in a deliberative democracy. I support this sentiment (as I think many educators would) but want to exercise caution in how we might frame the discussion. If the so-called problem is that young adults do not vote, then we see them as the problem that we need to fix. Thus, we frame our classes to show and/or tell them how important it is to vote and then curse them for perceived inadequacies come the next election or when we discuss whatever recent political snafu that has just occurred. Biesta (2010) advocated for looking towards what might be educational about education—namely, that education is more than qualification (e.g., learning how voting works) and socialization (e.g., how students might fit into existing structures like political parties). Education is about subjectification—becoming a subject (e.g., exploring about how systems of voting can privilege some folks, and oppress others, and our roles within those systems). My colleague, Kent den Heyer, and I understand subjectification as related to the ethics of fidelity Badiou describes (den Heyer & van Kessel, 2015). Instead of learning facts or how to acquiesce to a social norm, becoming subjects must think independently and act ethically as the proceed with the truths they encounter (i.e., avoiding disaster):

> There is always only one question in the ethic of truths: how will I, as some-one, continue to exceed my own being? How will I link the things I know, in a consistent fashion, via the effects of being seized by the not-known? (Badiou, 1993/2001, p. 50)

How might we shift to a more affirmative sense of citizenship? Badiou's philosophy of evil can potentially increase students' sense of agency in the sociopolitical sphere. Firstly, Badiou's secular understanding of evil not only squarely places violence and cruelty in the human sphere, but also highlights that ordinary humans are indeed capable of contributing to good and evil. Secondly, we are encouraged to remain faithful to our truth procedures. Thirdly, we can develop our theories of change to include an interconnected, but individual responsibility to work towards breaking barriers—specifically those barriers that limit the potential for fidelity among those arbitrarily labelled as different. There is no specific framework to follow of what to do or how to do it, just a set of ethics to help us persevere.

Affirmative stances are tricky in philosophy of education (and elsewhere), but potentially fruitful. In this task, I seek guidance from Naomi Hodgson, Joris Vlieghe, and Piotr Zamojski's *Manifesto for a Post-Critical Pedagogy* (2017). In this brief but powerful manifesto, they articulated five principles, namely: there are indeed principles, even though these are not prescriptive; the challenges from dwelling together in a common world do not have to divide us; equality and transformation are possible; hope in the present can be a basis for education; and instead of education for citizenship, we might shift to "love for the world" (pp. 15–19). We ought not to indoctrinate students into existing modes of being, or dictate what they ought to do:

In current formulations, taking care of the world is framed in terms of education *for* citizenship, education *for* social justice, education *for* sustainability, etc. in view of a particular notion of global citizenship and an entrepreneurial form of intercultural dialogue. Although perhaps underpinned by a progressive, critical pedagogy, the concern in such formulations of responsibility for the world is with ends external to education. (Hodgson, Vlieghe, & Zamojski, 2017, p. 18)

These principles do not dissolve the differences that harm us—ethnoracism, sexism and misogyny, ableism, economic disparity, among others. Instead, there is opportunity (and, dare I say, hope): we can affirm what we might do in the present, while accepting that the youths we are teaching will act according to their own sense of being in the world.

REFERENCES

Arendt, H. (1998). *The human condition* (2nd ed.). Chicago, IL: University of Chicago Press. (Original work published in 1958)

Badiou, A. (2001). *Ethics: An essay on the understanding of evil* (P. Hallward, Trans.). London, UK: Verso. (Original work published in 1993)

Badiou, A., & Tarby, F. (2013). *Philosophy and event* (L. Burchill, Trans.). Malden, MA: Polity Press. (Original work published in 2010)

Barbour, C. A. (2010). Militants of truth, communities of equality: Badiou and the ignorant schoolmaster. *Educational Philosophy and Theory, 42*(2), 251–263. https://doi.org/10.1111/j.1469-5812.2008.00488.x.

Bartlett, A. (2006). The pedagogical theme: Alain Badiou and an event-less education. *AntiTHESIS, 16*, 129–147.

Bartlett, A. (2011). *Badiou and Plato: An education by truths.* Edinburgh, Scotland: Edinburgh University Press.

Biesta, G. (2010). *Good education in an age of measurement: Ethics, politics, democracy.* Boulder, CO: Paradigm.

Burgan, M. (2010). *Refusing to crumble: The Danish resistance in World War II.* Mankato, MN: Compass Point.

Byers, M. (2012). *Intent for a nation: What is Canada for? A relentlessly optimistic manifesto for Canada's role in the world.* Vancouver, Canada: Douglas & McIntyre.

Critchley, S. (2012). *The faith of the faithless: Experiments in political theology.* New York, NY: Verso.

Dąbrowski, K. (1964). *Positive disintegration.* Boston, MA: Little Brown.

den Heyer, K. (2009). Education as an affirmative invention: Alain Badiou and the purpose of teaching and curriculum. *Educational Theory, 59*, 441–463.

den Heyer, K. (2014, September 14). Badiou and the educational situation. *Politics and Culture*. Retrieved from https://politicsandculture. org/2014/09/01/badiou-and-the-educational-situation-by-kent-den-heyer/.

den Heyer, K. (2015). An analysis of aims and the educational "event". *Canadian Journal of Education, 38*(1), 1–27.

den Heyer, K., & Conrad, D. (2011). Using Alain Badiou's ethic of truths to support an 'eventful' social justice teacher education program. *Journal of Curriculum Theorizing, 27*(1), 7–19. Retrieved from http://journal.jctonline.org/index.php/jct/article/view/302/95.

den Heyer, K., & van Kessel, C. (2015). Evil, agency, and citizenship education. *McGill Journal of Education, 50*(1), 1–18. Retrieved from http://mje.mcgill. ca/issue/view/556.

Gaudelli, W. (2003). *World class: Teaching and learning in global times*. London, England: Lawrence Erlbaum.

Hallward, P. (2013, July 22). Radical thinkers: Alain Badiou's ethics—Video. *The Guardian*. Retrieved from https://www.theguardian.com/commentisfree/ video/2013/jul/12/alain-badiou-ethics-video-radical-thinkers.

Hodgson, N., Vlieghe, J., & Zamojski, P. (2017). *Manifesto for a post-critical pedagogy*. Earth, Milky Way: punctum.

Office of the High Commissioner for Human Rights. (1948). *Universal declaration of human rights*. Retrieved from http://www.ohchr.org/EN/UDHR/ Pages/Language.aspx?LangID=eng.

Parker, W. C. (2003). *Teaching democracy: Unity and diversity in public life*. New York, NY: Teacher's College Press.

Pinar, W. (2011). *The character of curriculum studies*. New York, NY: Palgrave.

Richardson, G. H. (2002). *The death of the good Canadian: Teachers, national identities and the social studies curriculum*. New York, NY: Peter Lang.

Schmidt, S. J. (2010). Civic education curriculum. In C. Kridel (Ed.), *Encyclopedia of curriculum studies* (pp. 109–110). Thousand Oaks, CA: SAGE.

Smith, B. A. (2006). The limits of the subject in Badiou's *Being and Event*. In P. Ashton, A. J. Bartlett, & J. Clemens (Eds.), *The praxis of Alain Badiou* (pp. 71–101). Melbourne, Australia: re.press.

Spector, H. (2015). The who and the what of educational cosmopolitanism. *Studies in Philosophy and Education, 34*, 423–440.

Spector, H. (2017). The cosmopolitan subject and the question of cultural identity: The case of *Crime and Punishment*. *Crime, Media, Culture: An International Journal, 13*, 21–40.

Strahan, A. (2010). The obliteration of truth by management: Badiou, St. Paul and the question of economic managerialism in education. In Kent den Heyer (Ed.), *Thinking education through Alain Badiou* (pp. 78–98). New York, NY: Wiley-Blackwell.

Taubman, P. M. (2010). Alain Badiou, Jacques Lacan and the ethics of teaching. *Educational Philosophy and Theory, 42*(2), 196–212. https://doi.org/10.1111/j.1469-5812.2009.00532.x.

United Nations Office on Drugs and Crime. (2013). *Human Trafficking.* Retrieved from http://www.unodc.org/unodc/en/human-trafficking/what-is-human-trafficking.html.

Westheimer, J., & Kahne, J. (2004). What kind of citizen? The politics of educating for democracy. *American Educational Research Journal, 41,* 237–269.

Willinsky, J. (1998). *Learning to divide the world: Education at empire's end.* Minneapolis: University of Minnesota Press.

CHAPTER 5

The Politics of Evil

The *politics of evil* refers to an invocation of evil in political rhetoric against a person or group that, intentionally or otherwise, stifles democratic debate, and can promote hate speech such as George W. Bush's reference to the "Axis of Evil." Labelling a group as evil taps into powerful imagery from religion, popular media, and other cultural sources. Drawing from a qualitative study with Grade 11 students and the concept of order-words from Deleuze and Guattari, this chapter examines the power the label of evil has in the context of the study of historical and contemporary events.

THE POWER OF EVIL

What conceptions of evil do secondary school students hold? In subjects such as history, literature, and social studies, among others, students examine historical events rife with large-scale violence often labelled as evil (e.g., genocide) as well as political rhetoric that evokes evil, such as Reagan's "evil empire" in the context of the Cold War or G. W. Bush's "Axis of Evil" during discussions of the War on Terror. Evil is not a word that

---

An earlier version of this chapter was published as: van Kessel, C. (2017). "A Phenomenographic Study of Youth Conceptualizations of Evil: Order-Words and the Politics of Evil," *Canadian Journal of Education, 40*(4), 329–355.

© The Author(s) 2019
C. van Kessel, *An Education in 'Evil'*,
Palgrave Studies in Educational Futures,
https://doi.org/10.1007/978-3-030-16605-2_5

84   C. van KESSEL

is easily conceptualized, yet the impact of this word permeates our lives here in Canada and elsewhere. There are, of course, stereotypes that rely on a simplistic binary of good versus evil, but the real power lies not with identifying a specific representation or definition of evil, but with how the word and concept of evil can operate (see Youngblood Jackson, 2013). In this study, I purposefully interviewed students without providing them with a definition of evil because it is clear from the philosophical and psychological literature that the definition is up for debate. Regardless of how evil might be defined by youths (e.g., sadism, putrid defilement, bureaucratic thoughtlessness), my research points to affects (bodily) and effects (cognitive) of contempt when someone or something is labelled as evil. I then examine some of the implications these affects and effects have for political literacy. For this chapter, I am limiting my discussion to participant responses, and, specifically, to how Deleuze and Guattari's order-words are helpful for my more specific purpose of demystifying political rhetoric of evil, a key theme that emerged.

According to Gilles Deleuze and Félix Guattari (1980/2008), language can transform us, not physically, but in terms of our social position, or how we interact with others (Bryant, 2011, para. 7). For example, when a judge deems someone "guilty," the verdict changes a *person* into a *convict*. There is an "incorporeal transformation" that involves a change in *status* of a body or the change in its *relations* to other bodies; for example, when this person is on trial, the proceedings and the sentencing directly affect the body and its relationship to other bodies, most notably being "the transformation of the accused into a convict [as] a pure instantaneous act or incorporeal attribute that is expressed in the judge's sentence" (Deleuze & Guattari, 1980/2008, pp. 80–81). Also, a convict's physical body is confined and submitted to not only a prison routine but also the accompanying threats to that body within the structure. Order-words are "not a particular category of explicit statements (for example, in the imperative), but the relations of every word or every statement to implicit presuppositions" (Deleuze & Guattari, 1980/2008, p. 79). Basically, order-words are not grammatically a specific type of command; rather, they have the thrust of a command because of the assumptions they both tap into and create. They are like passwords—they simultaneously give power and take it away. Order-words can shut down freedom and even the act of thinking itself, and thus are distinctly political and relevant to social studies.

Evil is an order-word. This word morphs an ordinary human into a *villain*. The application of the word "evil," like the word "guilty," can change social positions in a profoundly negative way. In the context of social studies education, evil as an order-word is particularly relevant to issues of political rhetoric. The invocation of evil can have catastrophic consequences. An extreme example would be Hitler's description in *Mein Kampf* (1925/2001) that "the personification of the devil as the *symbol of all evil* assumes the living shape of the Jew" (p. 293, emphasis added). The label of evil is its own force that influences what we think and what we do, and the invocation of evil in *Mein Kampf* facilitated the murder of millions of innocent people. I examined the variety of conceptualizations of evil held by secondary school students.

PHENOMENOGRAPHY OF EVIL

My research approach for this study was phenomenography, a qualitative methodology based on the ontological and epistemological assumptions that there is no objective, singular Truth or closed reality. Phenomenography's etymological roots are from the Greek noun φαινομενων (phainomenōn), referring to what has been acquired from appearance in a sensory experience or become mentally apparent, and γραφειν (graphein), the verb "to write" (Liddell & Scott, 1996, pp. 360 and 1913). Thus, through its roots, the research approach involves researchers writing down what participants sense or realize. Phenomenography, however, involves more than simply recording participants' interpretations. The researcher can focus on particular words and phrases to illuminate the analysis rather than being held to the entirety of the transcript. Having said that, it is important to remain faithful to the context of the quotations, attempting to avoid inserting the researcher's ideas into the participant responses. A "conception" in phenomenography has two intertwined aspects, referential and structural. The referential aspect refers to the meaning the subject places upon the object, while the structural aspect refers to the features the subject discerns and then focuses on, but both can relate to theoretical or physical experience (Marton & Pong, 2005; Wood et al., 2017). A sample group determines a range of possible ways to experience a phenomenon, not for an *individual* but for a *population*, in a specific context to which the sample belongs (Åkerlind, 2005, p. 323; Larsson & Holmström, 2007); thus, a phenomenographer does not catalogue responses of participants nor how many share that view (Peck, Sears, & Donaldson, 2008).

My attempt to capture experience is informed by Pitt and Britzman's (2003) apt identification of "the crisis of representation." Researchers attempt "to offer some contingent observations about how individuals—including the researcher—make knowledge in and of the world" in the context of trying to discern difficult knowledge with a poststructuralist humility regarding experience (p. 756). My study involved semi-structured individual interviews with a participant-generated stimulus, as well as a task-based focus group with the same participants, and then a follow-up set of individual interviews. I began the initial interviews with the creation of an image or text of what came to mind when participants first heard the word "evil." The use of a stimulus to provoke participants is a common feature of phenomenographic interviews (e.g., Löfström, Nevgi, Wegner, & Karm, 2015; Peck, 2010). I then asked open-ended questions that I had prepared in advance. Questions included:

- Are there other words you might use to convey the same meaning as "evil"?
- Do you think that people can be evil to their core or do you think that only actions are evil? If you can, describe some examples.
- What characteristics must someone or something possess to be evil?
- Do you see evil in historical or present events?
- Would you be surprised if you witnessed evil in your daily life?
- What do you think about presidents and prime ministers using the word evil in political speeches?

This project sought to explore a new topic in the hopes of provoking participants "into thinking about or seeing something differently" and thus fits into qualitative research that can "serve as an intervention, stimulate self-reflection, [and] generate social awareness" (Leavy, 2017, p. 6). In addition to individual interviews, I used focus groups because they can be helpful for ascertaining participant perceptions of issues (Ellefsen, 2016), particularly the extent to which concepts are difficult or easy to understand (Löfström, 2014), and where the subject matter is of a sensitive nature (Barbour 2007; Berg 2004; Stewart & Shamdasani, 1990). I asked groups of three to four participants to place images and text along a spectrum of more to less evil. I had planned on using the participant-created pictures from the initial interview; however, because participants generally did not draw pictures, I added images based on the written and verbal responses from the interviews as well as my own judgement with the intention of providing engaging stimuli for the task-based group activity to provoke "vibrant discussion about the phenomenon under study" (Peck, 2010, p. 585). These images included historical figures (Adolf Hitler, Pol Pot, Adolf Eichmann), fictional characters (a demon, Darth Vader, Voldemort, Nosferatu, Edward Cullen), non-human entities (Hurricane Katrina and Ebola), and short text descriptions (murderer who kills adults, murderer who kills children, person who accidently kills an adult, person who accidently kills a child). The group task provided an opportunity for participants to discuss evil with each other instead of answering my questions, which produced a more casual dynamic than the structured individual interviews because the participants could converse in a more "natural" way (Ellefsen, 2016, p. 164). After the focus group, I interviewed participants individually again. At that point, I asked them the extent to which they agreed with their group's placement of images and probed them regarding some claims arising from the earlier interviews.

Demographic Information

Interviews took place at a non-denominational, independent school with a population ranging from kindergarten through Grade 12 located in a major urban area in Western Canada. I am aware that my snapshot is of a specific place, time, and context, and thus, my findings do not preclude the existence of other categories.

Fifteen participants were drawn from the 2014–2015 Grade 11 (junior) class, aged 16–18 years old. I asked participants to self-identify their gender, religion, and geographical background. Nine self-identified as male and six as female. Religious self-identification included Agnostic, Christian, Hindu, Muslim, Roman Catholic, Sikh, and Unitarian. All participants had been born in Canada, but their parents and/or grandparents heralded from a diverse range of countries: Canada, China, England, Germany, the Philippines, India, Iran, Iraq, Kuwait, Pakistan, Poland, Turkey, and the United States.

Analysis

Phenomenographers organize data into categories of description, an "outcome space" that corresponds to different meanings or ways of

88   C. van KESSEL

experiencing the phenomenon, as well as the logical "structural relationships linking these different ways of experiencing" (Åkerlind, 2005, p. 322). Following Marton (1981, 1986, 2015), I began with selected quotations from a variety of interviews, which I then decontextualized into a pool of meaning (Kettunen & Tynjälä, 2017). After reading through the transcripts, I composed a few obvious categories about evil and then analysed the transcripts accordingly, revising and creating new categories. My process was a reflexive and theorizing activity (Åkerlind, 2005; Belt & Belt, 2017; Marton, 1986; Marton & Booth, 1997). I identified and described similarities and variations, thus establishing the structural aspect (Marton & Pong, 2005). My final step was to reread all the transcripts looking for refinements to my analysis (Bowden & Green, 2010).

In phenomenography, attention to credibility (as opposed to a more modernist sense of "validity") is important throughout a study—the task is to respect participant responses, not pinpoint a truth. Paying attention to credibility includes fostering an openness to unique participant conceptualizations, selecting an appropriate group, negotiating meaning with the participants, defending the interpretation of the results persuasively, and ensuring dependability regarding the interview conversation and transcription (Collier-Reed, Ingerman, & Berglund, 2009, pp. 345–348; Guba & Lincoln, 2013, p. 59). Because my own "voice" will permeate the study, which has been shaped by "the framework of the social, cultural, historical, political, economic, ethnic, and gender positions of the constructor" (Guba & Lincoln, 2013, pp. 57–58), there can be no true objectivity due to inherent factors such as bias, judgement, and prejudice. Instead, there is a higher standard of objectivity, one that requires the recognition of subjectivities and their impact on research. Such *situated knowledges* (Haraway, 1988; Lang, 2011) require researchers to discuss how they are positioned and then seek knowledges that are translatable across subjective locations. I included member-checking with participants in the final individual interviews as well as continual efforts to separate my assumptions from those of my participants; however, "any outcome space is inevitably partial, with respect to the hypothetically complete range of ways of experiencing a phenomenon" (Åkerlind, 2005, p. 328).

Student Understandings of Evil

It was important for me to assure the student participants that I was not looking for a "right" answer. I just wanted to know what and how they think about evil and that I was not making any judgements about those ideas, nor did I need them to provide me with evidence for a claim I wanted to make. I informed them of this and told them that I simply wanted them to articulate their thoughts, and that whatever they said would be valuable to me. Participants visibly relaxed when I explained these things to them. Given that the goal was to map the range of conceptions that emerge in the group/individual settings, I also reassured them that I would not be "assigning" a conception to any one student. In other words, when the transcripts were to be analysed, I would be talking about the students as a whole and would not be pinning any conception to a particular person. This assurance seemed also to be of comfort to the participants.

Participants in this study provided an impressive range of conceptualizations of evil, many of which are interconnected with each other. I separated these into five referential aspects: evil as images; evil as affects (bodily) and effects (cognitive); evil as abnormal and extraordinary; evil as distinctly human; and evil as subjective. These aspects (e.g., differences in overall conceptualizations) revealed a variety of ways youths might think about evil. The first two categories—images and affects/effects—reveal what/how one might envision or experience evil. I consider these to be more "gut reactions" in the sense that they are often first responses and not over-intellectualized. The latter three categories—evil as abnormal, human, and subjective—speak to how one might define evil beyond these initial reactions (although not necessarily). Within each of these categories, there were variations (structural aspects of each referential aspect).

Evil as Images

Images participants conjured up were often religious in nature, such as the Devil and evil spirits. These images overlap with tropes from religion and horror films. Participants also included what is hidden, a secret, or part of the occult, as well what is considered geometrically or aesthetically flawed. The latter two subcategories relate to other frequent images of evil—darkness/the unknown, as well as ugliness. There is power inherent in the word evil:

> SERENA: I feel like evil is such an extreme word that nothing really matches it. It's a shooting word; it's just loaded. It's taking it to a whole new level. It takes it to a religious aspect as well somewhat because like evil is traditionally rooted from Satan and all that religious stuff; so it's a really loaded term and nothing really matches it.

For Nick, the image that popped into his head when he heard the word evil was "a devil with horns on his head, doing bad things to innocent people, getting others to do selfish things." Nikolai wrote: "sharp, jagged, harsh, often darkness" at the beginning of his interview and then described what he meant in more detail:

> As a representation of that, something that is geometrically flawed that is not physically possible has that strong connotation of evil in my mind. I've seen representations of this in video games and things like that, that try to portray evil using unclear physical boundaries and just the idea of distortion. This goes back to the idea of darkness. It's not really darkness per se, but it's obscurity and the inability to see what's going on.

When asked about what makes vampires evil, Kunta replied, "they can harm you, they are sinister, they have their cloaks and keep hidden, you don't know them, they come out at night, a time of darkness, you can't see—the unknown." The occult, literally "what is hidden" from the Latin *occultus* (Simpson, 1968, p. 408), is unmistakably associated with evil, as are those who are on the fringes of society. Drawing from an example of witch hunts, women, especially older wise ones, were frequently associated with the Devil and the occult. Serena, much to her own surprise, found herself drawing heavily from Disney movies, particularly *The Little Mermaid* and the character of Ursula:

> It's automatically what I think of. And I find it interesting that all the evil people in Disney are always old and ugly, and they always put them out to be women, and never men. It's always an older female. It's just the stereotype kind of.

In this study, Serena was unique in her identification of a gendered aspect of evil; however, it is perhaps unsurprising given the dominant gendered relations here in Canada (and elsewhere) within which women are to be desirable and alluring, and thus, older and/or independent women are objects of fear and revulsion (e.g., Anderson, 2015; Hester, 1992). The trope of evil as ugly did reappear in the transcripts with different participants and is also not new to Western social views. The ancient Greeks had a saying, καλός κ'αγαθός (kalos kagathos), which is often translated as "the beautiful and the good" (Liddell &

Scott, 1996).[1] Those who fit societal standards of attractiveness were assumed to have an equally good character or level of ability. Sociologists have noted this as a significant cognitive bias in play, dubbed the halo effect—the tendency to rate attractive people more favourably in terms of their other characteristics (Lachman & Bass, 1985; Thorndike, 1920). Conversely, unattractive people are assumed to have negative characteristics (Fabello, 2013). It is likely that none of these representations are shocking—they correspond with much popular media. Perhaps more interesting is not what represents evil, but how these representations affect us.

Evil as Affects (Bodily) and Effects (Cognitive)

It became clear from participant descriptions that evil can have a physical and psychological sensory component. This evil feeling is profoundly negative, which contributes to explanations as to why the rhetoric of evil in politics and elsewhere can be so powerful. Strawberry's feeling of evil did not take corporeal form, but rather indicated bodily affect:

> When I think of evil, I think of evil spirits; more like, you are walking down in the middle of the night somewhere, probably coming back from a friend's party, coming to your home, and all of a sudden there is this big gust of wind passing by and you feel that there is something wrong. And then you have a feeling that there is evil lurking around you... You feel really cold. It's so weird. You have a really strong feeling that something is present and you are actually being haunted or something.

At one point, Nikolai described evil as "a general feeling" that was linked to the anxiety of the "unknown" and "darkness," while Kunta noted that evil is linked to being "scared" when confronted with the "unknown" or by those who "are doing something to harm you." Thus, although there are clear images of evil, there are also feelings and sensations of evil. As

---

[1] καλός κ ἀγαθός (full form: καλός και αγαθός) is the masculine, singular, nominative form, and thus, the endings of the words would be different when referring to: other genders, in the plural, or when the phrase functions differently in a sentence (e.g., the nominative form as the subject of the sentence versus the accusative form as the object in a sentence).

92   C. van KESSEL

such, conjuring up such representations and bodily affects can be particularly impactful when evil is invoked in political rhetoric.

Evil as Distinctly Human (Mostly)

Interconnected patterns emerged from participant responses to questions about whether plants, non-human animals, and natural disasters can be evil. Participants generally identified evil as confined to humans, such as Kira saying that "Ebola and Katrina are just things." Some of this was attributed to an anthropocentric viewpoint as well as a lack of knowledge about animals, such as Riley remarking jovially that his "view is pretty humanity-centric, mostly because I'm a human." Jean emphasized that: "animals can be cruel... [but] I believe that evil is completely a human construct." Although Tom attributes his similar view to lack of knowledge ("we don't know that much about what goes on the minds of animals"), Amnis saw a similar, but more nuanced point of view:

> I guess not really because we aren't really sure what goes through the brain of an animal. Most times we think it's kind of like instinct. But then you get to like where otters rape baby seals to death. Is that evil? Or is that a weird nature thing like instinct? Is it a by-product of instinct maybe? I guess for animals and especially plants, you can't say they are evil, but when you get to things that have more intelligence, like chimps and stuff, they kind of do realize what they are doing, the consequences, then maybe you can kind of start using the label evil there because they do realize what's going to happen. They have a basic understanding of that. And if they still do something they know will cause harm to another chimp then maybe you can maybe label that as evil.

Participants saw evil as largely confined to the human realm because they understood the cognition involved in the criteria of evil (i.e., awareness and intention) as limited to humans. Such an anthropocentric view is interesting given the frequent association of evil and animality in popular film and television (e.g., werewolves) as well as the assumption of malign intent for some animals, such as the shark from *Jaws* (Spielberg, 1975). When these participants pondered the creatures in their ordinary lives, they seemed to subscribe to the Enlightenment worldview that only human animals are capable of reason, and such an assumption trumped the representations of evil.

For someone to be considered evil, they must make a choice to take that path and not be coerced into it. Tom and I spoke about the issue of intent:

> TOM: One of the first things that come to mind [when I hear "evil"] is the intent to hurt or destroy others, especially selfishly. I think that would be evil.... the intent to hurt or destroy others that could perhaps mean someone, who personally of his own volition, believes that he has to kill or harm others; that would be one category. Another category might be selfish sadism, enjoying in seeing others being hurt. People with a destructive personality who have no reason or motive for being that way, or some malicious motive.

Of course, in order to make that choice, an evil-doer must first be aware that their action is potentially evil, and then intend to do it; for example, a participant wrote "designed intentionally to inflict pain," and later in the interview made this comment about vampires:

> NIKOLAI: I mean you can think he's evil because he kills people, but that's just our bias because we are people. We don't consider ourselves evil because we eat animals. It's the same thing as long as there is no intent, no sadist intent.

Cold, rational intent was a common theme among participants.

> SERENA: If it was self defense and you kill someone, that wouldn't be bad but it wouldn't be good. But first-degree murder would be evil because you planned it and it's not like a spur of the moment kind of thing. If it's planned out and purposeful it's evil.

Because participants tended not to see natural disasters or animals as capable of intending (or even being aware of) evil, that disqualifies them from being classified as evil, even if their death toll is significant:

> NICK: I'm just finding this interesting about Ebola and Hurricane Katrina. Even though they may kill more people than these people will, even if they did that, I think we would still see these people as more of a threat to society, more evil. Basically, society thinks that these guys [Pol Pot, Hitler] are more evil than this because they have control over their actions, while these are just natural things.

Ebola and Katrina both killed on a grand scale and killed children, so what is the difference? Estavan responded that, "These are actual people, they have control over their actions." Participants staunchly conceived of both awareness and intent as inherently human capabilities; linking those two attributes with evil, the supposed uniqueness of human animals seems to be assumed. A possible implication of this finding would be an exploration of how we, as humans, navigate our both symbiotic and precarious relationships vis-à-vis other animals, as well as smaller entities such as bacteria and viruses.

Evil as Subjective

Most participants spoke to an idea that what we label as "evil" is subjective and that evil is created by nurture (or lack thereof), not nature:

> KUNTA: It's all really subjective. I think it's a good thing that we have things like the Devil/Satan/Lucifer, which are kind of the ultimate evil; don't be like that. But then somebody does that to you, and then you are like "they are evil," but then you do it back, and they are like, "no, you are evil," and it becomes complicated.

Related to this idea is that the more you know about someone or something, the more difficult it is to label them as evil, as Martin articulated, "the backstory is just as important as the definition [of evil]... I mean, you can see it as an act of evil but it shouldn't be branded as evil without the full story, the context." Tom mentioned something similar, "What if the person has lived a very terrible life? What if the person had no choice? What if the person was pressured into it?" As Benedict succinctly stated, "I think people become evil. I think everybody has the potential to be good or evil in the constraints of their society. It seems like circumstances, the people around them, push them to be different." Amnis noted a similar process:

> I think it's how you were raised. Your environment, the one you've been brought up in. If you are kind of taught that it's OK to do these things, that doesn't make you evil. But if you are taught what's right and what's wrong—morals and stuff— then something else in your life pushes you to go against those things, maybe like Hitler. Maybe if he had gone to art school he wouldn't have had all that pent-up rage.

An assumption of statements such as Amnis's is that evil is not inherent to our being; it is created from certain circumstances.

Despite the agreed upon lack of a universal evil, certain interrelated attributes led some participants to label someone or something as evil, a tipping point that makes someone evil regardless of a participant's appreciation for the subjectivity of evil: choice, lack of remorse, sadistic pleasure, innocent victims, scale, and intensity. Participants developed ideas that went beyond awareness of, and intention for, evil. The sheer scale of harm done could also make someone evil. In their focus group, Amnis, Nick, and Estavan used two criteria—scale and intention—to separate some of the fictional characters on the spectrum of more to less evil. They rated Voldemort and Darth Vader as more evil than vampires due to the scale of their crimes: Vader destroyed an entire planet and its people, and Voldemort killed a significant number of people. Furthermore, both Vader and Voldemort harmed and killed children. Harming children is generally seen as particularly heinous and thus extreme even on a small scale. Estavan said: "It's more serious if it's a child because they still have more of their life ahead of them. But that still doesn't give them a reason to kill adults."

What, then, if the scale is relatively small? When asked about the possibility of isolated acts of evil, one participant stated after a long pause:

> SERENA: I think they have to do more than one thing to be considered evil—no, wait a sec. I'm thinking terms of rape. In terms of Hitler it was all systematic and he did a lot of them [evil deeds], but with rape you can do it once I would consider you evil. It's very circumstantial for me. Like if the event is powerful enough. Like I know killing one person is very powerful, but killing a lot of people sends a bigger message thinking of the sheer impact… If it's like a bunch of rapes by one person rather than one, it's obviously a huger impact than the one, but obviously just one still has a pretty big impact. And the same with murdering people.

Participants saw these actions (e.g., mass murder, rape) as extreme due to their particular scale (i.e., sheer number of victims) and/or intensity (i.e., severe impact on a limited number of victims). In such cases, even "good" intentions are trumped by extreme actions. The scale or intensity of an atrocity negates any positive intentions, thus still necessitating a label of evil. As Mary said, "I think your intentions are one of the most important things to make that difference, but it's also kind of what you do, like if it's something really bad then it's obviously going to be

96   C. van KESSEL

considered evil." In cases of this scale or intensity, even "good" intentions are trumped by extreme actions:

> MARTIN: [Hitler] had those good intentions, but by doing that to that extreme he was throwing away his humanity to pull off those orders of the genocide and all of that. So that evil is kind of different in my opinion.

Amnis echoed a similar sentiment: "Yeah, I guess he [Hitler] maybe did have good intentions to maybe get Germany out of its bad position, but like half the stuff he did he didn't have to do. So that's the tipping point toward evil."

Evil as Abnormal, Extraordinary

Participants overwhelmingly conceived evil as being at the individual level, but only extraordinary ones. Organizations can be evil, but that is dependent on the individuals within them. As Tom stated,

> Organizations are typically led by people. Al Qaeda was led by Osama Bin Laden; the Nazi party was led by Adolf Hitler. These organizations are based on the ideologies of the people who lead them or the people who founded them.

Evil, thus, can operate on a grand scale, but at the heart of it will be the individual human components and their actions. Benedict said:

> I think everyone actually sees it as individual because it's just our nature. We need some kind of face to put to something. Like when we think of Apple, the company, we think of Steve Jobs, you know? It's a face that's associated with a company or circumstances...like if you think of genocide in Germany then you think of Hitler. It's a face to put with a situation.

The problem with this hyper-individualization of broader structures and processes is that it can disperse accountability; it makes it difficult to see how individual actions are nested within, or made possible by, interconnected people working within larger structural and historical forces. As Britzman (1986) states, "The ideology which supports this notion of the rugged individual is used to justify success or failure, social class, and social inequality. This brand of individualism infuses the individual with both undue power and undue culpability" (p. 453; see also Britzman, 2003). Hyper-individualization of Hitler or any other historical villain runs contrary to recognizing the nexus of individual and community culpability (van Kessel & Crowley, 2017). In a follow-up interview with Nick, this issue became very clear when we spoke about how much we tend to pin blame on Hitler in relation to broader society:

> NICK: So, that's what I also think the Nazis did, maybe not exactly the Nazis maybe even the West as well, and like England and the U.S. Basically, I think this is what they did. Throughout our lives, even when we don't know anything about WWII, even when we are young, we know there's a guy called Adolf Hitler. Because he's like, people make us believe that he was the leader, which he was. He controlled everyone in his group to do the exact same things he did. So, it makes it look like he's controlling everyone. But I believe he didn't do that. Eichmann, for example, just the fact that he knows what this group is about and what Hitler does, too, makes him just as bad.

Nick clearly understands that the processes of evil instigated by the Nazis did not belong to a single villain. Hyper-individualization of Hitler or any other historical villain runs contrary to the nexus of individual and community culpability integral to the notion of the *banality of evil* (Arendt, 1963/2006), and relates to a process I have called *villainification* (see Chapter 3).

A particularly interesting finding was that participants considered evil to be unlikely in their own daily lives, and yet also recognized that what we might label as evil (e.g., processes in play during Nazi Germany) were part of those individuals' daily lives. In other words, evil is thought to be personally irrelevant. As Nikolai stated: "I would be surprised [to see evil in my daily life]… If I saw something bad I wouldn't be as surprised. If I saw something that I would genuinely consider evil it would be very shocking." Amnis echoed a similar sentiment: "It's kind of like, it's not like we live in a post-apocalyptic [world] or some place where there is anarchy or anything like that." It should, however, be noted that not all participants shared that view. Jean noted that, "of course, I would be startled and uncomfortable. But I do think that I could see evil anywhere."

98 C. van KESSEL

Related to this sentiment of evil seeming foreign to our daily lives is our sense of agency (or lack thereof) in combatting evil, as Serena explained:

> I would like to say [the Holocaust] wouldn't [happen again] because it's happened before. History does repeat itself, but we try to prevent it. But maybe I feel like it would. There is so much conflict in the world right now, I think it's bound to happen, especially somewhere like the Middle East or something... We always hear these stories of people like Malala [Yousafzai], she was one person who reached out to so many people, but it's such a hard thing these days for one person to make an impact. You feel so small. You need a bunch of people to actually make an impact, I feel. But then again there are those single people who make stuff happen. You need to be an icon already to have a voice, I feel. Like Angelina Jolie would be a lot easier than me doing it. It just wouldn't work for me; I'm a nobody.

Returning to the idea of hyper-individualization, this is another negative effect of seeing individuals as effecting change. Failing to recognize interconnections among ordinary folks behind major societal changes and events (for both "good" and "evil") can leave us with a feeling of disempowerment. A number of participants pondered whether or not we could do anything about evil we encounter:

> NIKOLAI: Is it really possible to visualize something that is considered a societal norm? It's easy for us to look back and say that this is really obvious now, but can we right now look and see exactly what is wrong with society at this moment?

> TOM: Like eugenics, right here in Alberta and many other places it was accepted an idea. This just shows the significance of how our perceptions change. Back then, people thought that this was going to be good. And that goes to show how we judge these things until long after they have happened. It's difficult with historical figures. These perceptions would change depending on which era you looked at them from.

Tom then added later, "humans are naturally myopic." This calls into question the criteria of awareness for evil and has implications for how we educate youths to foster thinking that is independent from authority.

Evil is not a term applied to ourselves; it is a critique reserved for other people. For example, when asked if she saw any labels of evil in historical events, Kunta paused and then replied:

> The first thought that came to mind was neo-Nazis. I'm personally against it, obviously. Because Hitler lost World War II, we see Hitler as the evil one, but if Hitler had won I'd probably see Jews as evil... it's about the majority view... it's not that there's evil and then there's the other people, there's evil and then there's us.

This idea interconnects the conceptualizations that evil is a matter of perspective and that the more the personal details you know, the harder it is to label someone as evil.

There are many implications of these webbed conceptualizations in education. From the referential aspect of evil as images, an analysis of pictures in textbooks is warranted. What pictures of figures like Adolf Hitler are chosen by authors and publishers, and what effect and affects do these representations have? What happens when students and teachers see an image of Hitler, sitting sternly in uniform? How might that change if they see pictures of him kissing babies, laughing while on the phone, or playing with dogs? Thinking more generally of the aspect of evil as affects and effects, how might images and textual descriptions of genocides and other horrific events produce sensations and feelings in students?

POLITICS OF EVIL

One of the implications from this study on youth conceptualizations of evil is the need to trouble the *politics of evil*. I have defined the politics of evil as the invocation of evil in political rhetoric against a person or group that (intentionally or not) stifles democratic debate, and can promote hate speech, such as George W. Bush's aforementioned reference to the Axis of Evil (Bush, 2002). In social studies, educators are generally expected to build students' political literacy skills and capacities for critical thinking. Thus, implications arose from my commitment at the beginning of my doctorate to think seriously about how educators might teach issues like war, genocide, and systemic racism in ways that produce feelings of agency and responsibility without descending into despair.

The politics of evil encourages obedience to political authority, and thus, the ability to deconstruct it is a meaningful form of political literacy—helping students to understand and navigate political rhetoric. The politics of evil is harmful to the process of thinking in a public sense—thinking independently from authority, but interconnected with others—because this rhetoric manipulates our bodily affects and cognitive effects of our nascent understandings of evil, creating an "us versus them" mentality more so than a critical engagement with policies and their effects. There is much wisdom in our bodies—in how we experience feelings and emotions—and such experiences can make learning with/through evil a generative option (e.g., Ndalianis, 2012; Thacker, 2011). The political manipulation of such affects and effects, in contrast, can be dangerous to good relations with others.

The consequences of political invocations of evil can be catastrophic, such as the death and suffering resulting from the U.S.-led wars in Afghanistan and Iraq, not to mention the proliferation of domestic policies that removes citizens' rights. The politics of evil can shift public attention away from government (in)actions and policies:

> AMNIS: I guess it's kind of twisting the word, especially Bush—the Axis of Evil, you know... [Politicians] are just using that towards their own needs, especially for Bush. It's much easier to become president in wartime and stay president. Like, you create an out group or an in group, it's much easier to control your in group, it's us versus them. It's a lot easier to control your own population. That stops people from pointing fingers at you.

This process of shutting down critical thought is partly because of the bodily affects and cognitive effects of evil. Kira spoke about the fear produced by naming someone or something as evil: "It kind of gives a notion of fear. So, if something is bad you don't necessarily have to be afraid of it. But if it's evil, it sounds terrifying." Anyone can tap into these feelings, but the impact can be more severe when a politician invokes evil:

> SERENA: Everyone believes what the prime minister and president say, because they are the leaders. So if they label terrorism as evil, then we are going to think that, and we won't want to back down or compromise. I think it hinders us from resolving issues... If you label it as evil, you are going to take it at face value, you are not going to dig deeper and see that we did this to them and that's why they are doing it back.

If a politician uses the word evil in a speech, those who hear the speech might take it as a given, rather than questioning it in a critical way as we might with a peer.

The use of the term and the concept of evil produces an intensity that can influence our assumptions and actions in terms of our social position, or how we interact with others (Deleuze & Guattari, 1980/2008). I asked participants how they would react differently if I said, "Watch out for that guy, he's evil," versus "Watch out for that guy, he's bad." Estavan responded: "Well, if he's bad, I'd just think more that he's rude, he's impolite, whereas if you said evil I'd be more suspicious about him." To reiterate Kunta's quote from earlier: "...it's not that there's evil and then there's the other people, there's evil and then there's *us*" (emphasis added). Evil and otherness are intimately entwined. "We" can never be evil—such a term is reserved for those whom we deem as not belonging, which, of course, can never be us. Kira noted:

> It's like, through the years, evil is portrayed as the one you are against politically usually. So, it's like those [World War II] cartoons we watched where the bad guys were like Japanese people with bad teeth and stuff. And then they were evil because they were ugly. Oh yeah—evil and ugly. They always make the pretty person good and the ugly person evil. [Characters in Disney movies] are also ugly and they have big noses. I heard that some of them might be a thing to attach to the Jews.

The order-word of evil shapes our interactions with the groups and the objects that are associated with them (symbols, etc.), and we use stereotypes and prejudices to justify our assumptions. The naming of evil has profound implications for how that body is treated, where that body is considered legitimately to be, and the intents ascribed to that body's actions. Here lies a link between evil and hate. When a group who is an "other," i.e., those who do not conform to the norms of a particular society (by choice or by default), the label of evil can very easily incite hate speech, and thus discrimination and violence. By associating an "other" (in Kira's example, the Jews) with evil, there can be a tremendous intensity that affects us both consciously and unconsciously, and thus, we can easily fall into the trap of racism. The conception of evil then shapes our interactions with these groups of "others." The evil group, the villains, can now more easily be denied even the most basic of rights—what we are willing to do to villains versus those we consider to be fellow human beings is profoundly different.

102   C. van KESSEL

These processes are constantly in play. An Internet search of "evil" in January 2016 revealed a Yahoo Answers section on "Why are Muslims so evil?" with 30 answers (Anonymous, n.d.). The so-called best answer cites violent passages from the Quran, listing those who Muhammad supposedly killed. This answer was posted in 2011 and has garnered many comments over the years, some critical of the author (and the question itself), while other comments are clearly hate speech, powered by the effects and affects of evil, such as:

> [Muslims] complain about their own lands. Move to those of others, scream RACIST every time anyone complains and try to make that land like the one they left. *They're evil and should be exterminated.* Every group should recognise that these people are a disease on the earth that must be eliminated.

The roots of this hate speech may have been influenced by the exacerbated climate of hate against Muslims since 9/11, likely stemming from both political rhetoric and popular culture. In such cases of hate speech, evil is invoked with potentially tragic consequences. Critical thoughtfulness becomes diminished through the political rhetoric of fear. My participants did not necessarily disagree with the label of evil; for example, many thought it was appropriate to label the Islamic State of Iraq and the Levant (ISIL) as evil; however, a few participants were wary of the political and social repercussions, such as anti-Muslim hate speech and violence, as well as a failure to examine systemic issues that caused a group like ISIL to emerge in the first place. As Carlson (1985) noted, it is easy to distort a complex situation when it is presented in "an uncontested, taken-for granted manner" (p. 58). As I understand it, one of the main messages of the participant responses from this study is to use the label of evil with caution. This conclusion mirrors Stanley's (1999) attention to detail when deciding how to teach his children about the Nazis. Word choice is important, including vocabulary and verb tense, as is careful thought regarding the consequences of the content and its delivery.

CONCLUSIONS

Participants provided a range of conceptualizations of evil. Some focused on what they visualized, and some reflected on what they felt. They spoke thoughtfully about evil as being extraordinary and abnormal, and participants did not have the expectation of witnessing or taking part in something evil. This understanding is particularly heightened in historical contexts; for example, it seemed easier to label events in the past more so than contemporary ones. Participants did not generally see plants and animals as capable of evil, and when they did, those animals' awareness and thus intent for evil were assumed to be on par (or close to on par) with humans. In many contexts, participants saw evil as subjective—that evil is a matter of personal or societal perspective. The more you know about people, the less likely you would be to label them as evil, and this understanding partially explains why it might be so difficult to label those in our daily lives as evil.

Regardless of specific understandings of evil, this study made clear the power that the order-word of evil has, particularly in political rhetoric. By identifying and then troubling the power of this word, there is an opportunity to add meaningful and important complexity to social studies classrooms. Educators in classrooms can spark discussions about the complex people and processes involved, as well as our own senses of evil and what might be produced by them. These discussions can be a helpful form of political literacy, developing independent thinkers who might challenge the simplistic politics of fear and hate, and instead engage with more nuanced perspectives. Thus, it behooves educators, curriculum designers, and textbook authors and editors to think about whether their classroom resources and practices exacerbate or thwart the politics of evil. By assessing the bodily affects and cognitive effects that the word evil has as an order-word, students and teachers can guard against these dangerous political invocations.

REFERENCES

Åkerlind, G. S. (2005). Variation and commonality in phenomenographic research methods. *Higher Education Research & Development, 24,* 321–334. https://doi.org/10.1080/07294360.2011.642845.

Anderson, K. J. (2015). *Modern misogyny: Anti-feminism in a post-feminist era.* Oxford, UK: Oxford University Press.

Anonymous. (n.d.). Why are Muslims so evil? *Yahoo Answers.* Retrieved from https://ca.answers.yahoo.com/question/index?qid=20120309021220AAH 26DR.

Arendt, H. (2006). *Eichmann in Jerusalem: A report on the banality of evil.* New York, NY: Penguin. (Original work published in 1963)

Barbour, R. (2007). *Doing focus groups.* London, UK: Sage.

104   C. van KESSEL

Belt, A., & Belt, P. (2017). Teachers' differing perceptions of classroom disturbances. *Educational Research, 59,* 54–72.

Berg, B. (2004). *Qualitative research methods for the social sciences.* Boston, MA: Pearson.

Bowden, J. A., & Green, P. J. (2010). Relationality and the myth of objectivity in research involving human participants. In J. Higgs, N. Cherry, R. Macklin, & R. Ajjawi (Eds.), *Researching practice: A discourse on qualitative methodologies* (pp. 105–121). Rotterdam, The Netherlands: Sense.

Britzman, D. P. (1986). Cultural myths in the making of a teacher: Biography and social structure in teacher education. *Harvard Educational Review, 56,* 442–457.

Britzman, D. P. (2003). *Practice makes practice: A critical study of learning to teach* (Rev. ed.). New York, NY: State University of New York.

Bryant, L. R. (2011, February 20). Two types of assemblages. *Larval Subjects.* Retrieved from https://larvalsubjects.wordpress.com/2011/02/20/two-types-of-assemblages/.

Bush, G. W. (2002, January 29). State of the union address. *Presidential speeches archive.* Charlottesville, VA: Miller Center. Retrieved from https://millercenter.org/the-presidency/presidential-speeches/january-29-2002-state-union-address.

Carlson, D. (1985). The cold war in the curriculum. *Educational Leadership, 42,* 57–60.

Collier-Reed, B. I., Ingerman, Å., & Berglund, A. (2009). Reflections on trustworthiness in phenomenographic research: Recognizing purpose, context and change in the process of research. *Education as Change, 13,* 339–355.

Deleuze, G., & Guattari, F. (2008). *A thousand plateaus: Capitalism and schizophrenia* (B. Massumi, Trans.). London, UK: Continuum. (Original work published in 1980)

Ellefsen, L. (2016). An investigation into perceptions of Facebook use in higher education. *International Journal of Higher Education, 5,* 160–172. https://doi.org/10.5430/ijhe.v5n1p160.

Fabello, M. (2013, May 20). *Thin privilege* [Video web log post]. Retrieved from https://www.youtube.com/watch?v=qPETV_Jw1XU.

Guba, E. G., & Lincoln, Y. S. (2013). *The constructivist credo.* Walnut Creek, CA: Left Coast.

Haraway, D. (1988). Situated knowledges: The science question in feminism and the privilege of partial perspective. *Feminist Studies, 14,* 575–599.

Hester, M. (1992). *Lewd women and wicked witches: A study in the dynamics of male domination.* London, UK: Routledge.

Hitler, A. (2001). *Mein Kampf.* (R. Manheim, Trans.). Boston, MA: Houghton Mifflin. (Original work published in 1925)

Kettunen, J., & Tynjälä, P. (2017). Applying phenomenography in guidance and counselling research. *British Journal of Guidance and Counselling.* https://doi.org/10.1080/03069885.2017.1285006. (Advance online publication).

Lachman, S. J., & Bass, A. R. (1985). A direct study of the halo effect. *Journal of Psychology: Interdisciplinary and Applied, 119*(6), 535–540. https://doi.org/10.1080/00223980.1985.10542924.

Lang, J. C. (2011). Epistemologies of situated knowledges: "Troubling" knowledge in philosophy of education. *Educational Theory, 61,* 75–96.

Larsson, J., & Holmström, I. (2007). Phenomenographic or phenomenological analysis: Does it matter? Examples from a study on anaesthesiologists' work. *International Journal of Qualitative Studies on Health and Well-Being, 2,* 55–64.

Leavy, P. (2017). *Research design: Quantitative, qualitative, mixed methods, arts-based, and community-based participatory research approaches.* New York, NY: Guildford.

Liddell, H. G., & Scott, R. (1996). *A Greek-English lexicon.* Oxford, UK: Clarendon Press.

Löfström, J. (2014). How Finnish upper secondary students conceive transgenerational responsibility and historical reparations: Implications for the history curriculum. *Journal of Curriculum Studies, 46*(4), 515–539.

Löfström, E., Nevgi, A., Wegner, E., & Karm, M. (2015). Images in research on teaching and learning in higher education. In J. Huisman & M. Tight (Eds.), *Theory and method in higher education research* (Vol. 1, pp. 191–212). Bingley, UK: Emerald Group. https://doi.org/10.1108/S2056-375220150000001009.

Marton, F. (1981). Phenomenography: Describing conceptions of the world around us. *Instructional Science, 10,* 177–200. https://doi.org/10.1007/BF00132516.

Marton, F. (1986). Phenomenography: A research approach to investigating different understandings of reality. *Journal of Thought, 21,* 28–49. Retrieved from http://www.jstor.org/stable/42589189.

Marton, F. (2015). *Necessary conditions of learning.* New York, NY: Routledge.

Marton, F., & Booth, S. (1997). *Learning and awareness.* Hillsdale, NJ: Lawrence Erlbaum.

Marton, F., & Pong, W. Y. (2005). On the unit of description in phenomenography. *Higher Education Research & Development, 24,* 335–348. https://doi.org/10.1080/07294360500284706.

Ndalianis, A. (2012). *The horror sensorium.* Jefferson, NC: McFarland & Company.

Peck, C. (2010). "It's not like [I'm] Chinese and Canadian. I am in between": Ethnicity and students' conceptions of historical significance. *Theory and Research in Social Education, 38,* 574–617. https://doi.org/10.1080/0093 3104.2010.10473440.

Peck, C., Sears, A., & Donaldson, S. (2008). Unreached and unreasonable: Curriculum standards and children's understanding of ethnic diversity in Canada. *Curriculum Inquiry, 38,* 63–92. https://doi.org/10.1111/j.1467-873X.2007.00398.x.

106   C. van KESSEL

Pitt, A., & Britzman, D. P. (2003). Speculations on qualities of difficult knowledge in teaching and learning: An experiment in psychoanalytic research. *International Journal of Qualitative Studies in Education, 16,* 755–776. https://doi.org/10.1080/09518390310001632135.

Simpson, D. P. (1968). *Cassell's Latin dictionary.* New York, NY: Macmillan.

Spielberg, S. (Director). (1975). *Jaws* [Motion picture]. Universal City, CA: Universal Pictures.

Stanley, T. (1999). A letter to my children: Historical memory and the silences of childhood. In J. P. Robertson (Ed.), *Teaching for a tolerant world, Grades K-6: Essays and resources* (pp. 34–44). Urbana, IL: National Council for Teachers of English.

Stewart, D., & Shamdasani, P. (1990). *Focus groups: Theory and practice.* Newbury Park, CA: Sage.

Thacker, E. (2011). *In the dust of this planet.* Washington, DC: Zero.

Thorndike, E. L. (1920). A constant error in psychological ratings. *Journal of Applied Psychology, 4,* 25–29. https://doi.org/10.1037/h0071663.

van Kessel, C., & Crowley, R. M. (2017). Villainification and evil in social studies education. *Theory & Research in Social Education, 45,* 427–455. https://doi.org/10.1080/00933104.2017.1285734.

Wood, K., Jaidin, H., Jawawi, R., Perera, J. S. H. Q., Salleh, S., Shahrill, M., & Sithamparam, S. (2017). How and what teachers learn from collaborative professional development. *International Journal for Lesson and Learning Studies, 6,* 151–168. https://doi.org/10.1108/ijlls-09-2016-0028.

Youngblood Jackson, A. (2013). Posthumanist data analysis of mangling practices. *International Journal of Qualitative Studies in Education, 26,* 741–748.

CHAPTER 6

Symbolic Evil and the Schooling System

According to Jean Baudrillard, evil cannot be reduced to anything specific; rather, it is omnipresent. He calls this force *Symbolic Evil* in order to differentiate it from the common conception of moral evil. *Symbolic Evil* fuels metamorphosis and thus can be seen positively and negatively in great revolutionaries who tap into evil as the energy of challenge, defiance, creativity, and renewal. This chapter examines this concept in the context of Canadian and U.S. systems of schooling at the classroom, school, district, and national levels, noting the power of *Symbolic Evil* to help us redefine educational concerns like student "success."

JEAN BAUDRILLARD

Jean Baudrillard (1929–2007) was a French theorist who engaged in philosophy, social theory, and was a critic of what he saw as pressing issues in contemporary society and politics. After teaching in provincial *lycees* in France, he lectured in sociology at Paris Nanterre University. After retiring in 1987, he continued to write as well as present public lectures across the globe. He is sometimes referred to (and criticized as) the "high priest of postmodernism" for his contemporary focus as well as his "original style and extreme theorization of phenomena" (Merrin, 2007, para. 8). I would agree with identifying Baudrillard as a postmodernist if we understand postmodernism as Kip Kline (2016) does: "a lack of faith in Enlightenment projects and modern forms of dialectical critique"

© The Author(s) 2019
C. van Kessel, *An Education in 'Evil'*,
Palgrave Studies in Educational Futures,
https://doi.org/10.1007/978-3-030-16605-2_6

107

(p. 114). If, however, we take postmodernism in its often colloquial (and glib) sense of a time where truth and reality no longer matter, then I would disagree. Baudrillard's project was to defend the real, and yet as he noted, "the reality-fundamentalists... confus[e] message and messenger" (Baudrillard, 2004/2005, p. 23). He did not relish in the situations he described:

> Postmodernists didn't create the new fractured reality; they merely described it. The French academics of the 1970s, particularly Jean Baudrillard and Jean-Francois Lyotard, saw the flaws in modernist thought—that old-timey Enlightenment-era notion that we all shared values, approved the same truths, and agreed on facts. Instead, they acknowledged that reality is complicated. They recognized the changes happening in the late 20th century—the erosion of authority, the ascendance of individual perspective—and developed the vocabulary to describe it. (Livni, 2018, para. 4)

Baudrillard wrote on diverse subjects, most famously regarding his original critique of the "sign" system and our contemporary situation of simulacra and hyperreality. Simulations have become more real than reality itself, an idea which is applicable to education; for example, examining the fetishization of technology in schools in relation to the dissolution of reality (van Kessel & Kline, 2019) and how student disengagement might be attributed to our hyperreal situation as much as, or even more so than, personal characteristics (van Kessel, 2016). This chapter, however, focuses on his ideas about evil more so than specifically simulations and (a lack of) reality.

SYMBOLIC EVIL

Baudrillard contrasts many other thinkers in his conceptualization of evil. Instead of focusing on how evil happens or the role of intent, Baudrillard takes on the task of addressing evil itself. He makes an important distinction between evil as a force (*Symbolic Evil*) and evil in the vernacular sense of misfortunes (moral evil). There is a need to differentiate between *Symbolic Evil* (with an upper-case *E*, and also in this chapter in italics for clarity) and moral evil (with a lower-case *e*) in order to further our understanding of how these terms can be applied in a social context, specific in this case to education. *Evil* is a vital force of radical change that can reinvigorate our world and thus is neither good nor bad in itself.

Only time will tell whether that change will be deemed helpful or harmful. Moral evil is merely a bad or wholly negative outcome. *Evil* is an element of change; not merely the opposite of some supposed "good."

Evil diverts and reverses. It is also "intelligent... in the sense that it is implied automatically in every one of our acts" (Baudrillard, 2004/2005, p. 160). At any point, we can use or be used by this force. *Evil* cannot be reduced to anything in particular, but rather is ubiquitous in all things. In other words, *Evil* functions as both a verb and noun (i.e., it *functions* as much as it *describes*), simultaneously bridging the gap between the physical and metaphysical worlds. This interpretation entails that we cannot label a particular person or event as such, but instead *Evil* is embodied in any radical process of metamorphosis and becoming. As odd as it may sound, *Evil*, thus, understands us (rather than the other way around). *Evil* exposes humanity and all of its metaphorical warts by offering an opportunity to change and find meaning. This sense of *Evil* is then necessary to avoid stagnation, such as breaking artistic paradigms, or engaging in social activism, by offering alternatives to contemporary modes of being.

Such an idea runs directly contrary to many foundational philosophical understandings of evil. Immanuel Kant (1793/1838) interpreted evil as a product of rational choice, and thus, intent is of the utmost importance. There is a moral code—rigid, predetermined rules—that dictate whether humans are good or evil. Baudrillard, in contrast, conceptualizes an evil that is neither rational nor intentional. In fact, evil is not even "evil" in the sense of a misfortune, *Symbolic Evil* is neither good nor bad in itself, and it powers radical change. Perhaps the only similarity between Baudrillard and Kant is that evil is omnipresent, and the implications of this presence are very different. For Kant, humans are constantly fighting off evil, which is comprised of propensities and inclinations that are universally immoral, while for Baudrillard *Evil* is beyond simplistic framings of good or bad. *Evil* in this way is a deep-seated, pervasive force for dynamic change.

(Mis)Managing *Evil*

Society has been trying to control *Evil* and uncertainty in an effort to deny its radical alterity. *Evil* then is conceptualized as moral evil. Moral evil is what ought not to have been—a misfortune that can be relegated to the sidelines:

110   C. van KESSEL

once it has been exorcized by causes, misfortune is no longer a problem: it becomes susceptible of a causal solution and, above all, it originates elsewhere—in original sin, in history, in the social order, or in natural perversion. In short, it originates in an objectivity into which we exile it the better to be rid of it. (Baudrillard, 2004/2005, p. 152)

As such, evil can be thoughtlessly disregarded, becoming transparent instead of accepting the impossibility of understanding it. Although we think that we perceive evil (like seeing computer code), *Evil* can function without us knowing that it is happening. Meanwhile, societies expand and grow:

We are now governed not so much by growth as by growths. Ours is a society founded on proliferation, of growth which continues even though it cannot be measured against any clear goals. An excrescential society whose development is uncontrollable, occurring without regard for self-definition, where accumulation of effects goes hand in hand with the disappearance of causes. (Baudrillard, 1990/1993, p. 34)

Populations increase, governments expand territory, people use more and more natural resources and accumulate more objects. Concurrent to these growths is the attempt to eradicate evil. *Symbolic Evil* and moral evil are wiped from contemporary society because the "culture of global techno-modernity" enforces a "hegemonic culture of happiness" (Pawlett, 2014, §3, para. 2; cf. Baudrillard, 2004/2005, p. 139). We are commanded to be happy and enjoy. This culture reveals an "excess of positivity so exacerbated that negativity has been forbidden altogether" (Boldt-Irons, 2001, p. 84), thus creating an artificially antiseptic environment as we seek to expunge evil from the world. What is unpleasant becomes evil and, therefore, must be eliminated and never spoken of again in the present.

The Accursed Share

Modern Western society divided good and evil in the hopes of eliminating everything that hurts or harms us. As we have sought an antiseptic society free from evil, we have created an even more dangerous situation:

we become even more vulnerable to new forms of the accursed share that we secrete as a defense mechanism against a greater danger, the catastrophe of unchecked growth and a liberation that continues to radiate in all directions. This new form of accursed share is comprised of an energy source that is violent, that opposes, that resurrects what is other, what is foreign. (Boldt-Irons, 2001, p. 85; cf. Baudrillard, 1990/1993)

Baudrillard's use of the phrase "accursed share" stems from Georges Bataille's theory of consumption from his book, *The Accursed Share: An Essay on General Economy* (1949/1988). The accursed share is the excess, the superfluous energy, that must be vented in some way to avoid catastrophe. There is a choice to vent it through such things as artistic endeavours, nonprocreative sexuality, public spectacles, or through more extreme and catastrophic means such as war. There is a cosmic energy from the Sun as well as day-to-day chemical reactions that lies beyond simplistic calculations of profits and returns, especially considering it is impossible to expend all of this energy: some of it is destined for waste. Denying the existence of the accursed share is dangerous because it may be vented in ways that are destructive. The Romans recognized this situation, giving us the phrase "bread and circuses" as the emperors distracted the people with free food and gladiatorial games to vent the accursed share in a way that did not threaten the societal hierarchies that the elite sought to preserve. Thus, the accursed share can be manipulated by those in power to the detriment of those with less power; however, that situation can be reversed. Here lies the power of *Symbolic Evil*. If tapped into by those who might make radical (and hopefully eventually deemed beneficial) change, then the accursed share can be employed for the purposes of those changes. Instead of the accursed share being denied (with perhaps calamitous consequences) or being manipulated by the elite to maintain the status quo, it can accentuate the radical force of *Evil*. Although Baudrillard and Bataille disagree over where this excess of energy originates (Baudrillard, 1998), both agree that to deny the accursed share is dangerous. This denial is hazardous because, ironically, by seeking to eliminate misfortune and despair, we have created more. The management of evil has dispersed it throughout the world:

> [T]he anamorphosis of modern forms of Evil knows no bounds. In a society which seeks—by prophylactic measures, by annihilating its own natural referents, by whitewashing violence, by exterminating all germs and all of the accursed share, by performing cosmetic surgery on the negative—to concern itself solely with quantified management and with the discourse of the Good, in a society where it is no longer possible to speak Evil, Evil has metamorphosed into all the viral and terroristic forms that obsess us. (Baudrillard, 1990/1993, p. 81)

112   C. van KESSEL

Using a medical example to elucidate Baudrillard's thought, as a society we have been using superfluous antibiotics for a perceived threat, something we saw as evil and yet was merely a common virus that keeps our immune systems in check. By seeking to eliminate such threats, we have created superbugs immune to our antibiotics and thus wreaking havoc on our bodies and minds and revealing reality to be something other than what we believed or hoped.

The U.S.-led War on Terror is a case in point. Because antiseptic societies wish for no death, suicide bombers defeat the United States and their allies twice—by threatening society and then by removing the only equal reaction (to kill them). Furthermore, in the quest to prevent terrorism, more terrorists are created (i.e., by oppressing those believed to be threats). We might begin to fear not only those who are obvious terrorists but also those who appear inoffensive, we have transferred our symbolic fears onto others while attempting to remove them from our line of sight: any person, any plane could be a threat! In a constant state of vigilance and fear, there are few opportunities to enjoy what good we might have in our lives despite our superficial attempts to paint over our fears in order to only experience the positive. Terrorism is like a virus in a zero-sum game of death. By seeking to eliminate the evil of terrorism, where both extreme defiance and the equally extreme management of that defiance take an enormous toll.

Stockpiling the Past

Eliminating evil is not confined to contemporary events. Baudrillard argued that we stockpile our symbolic past to continually emphasis our "improvements" or ability to overtake our self-denied threats, but by doing so we cannot relieve ourselves of those existential threats:

> Our entire linear and accumulative culture would collapse if we could not stockpile the past in plain view.... We need a visible past, a visible continuum, a visible myth of origin to reassure us as to our ends, since ultimately we have never believed in them. (Baudrillard, 1983, pp. 19–20)

If the past is sanitized—our mistakes and malign actions fixed or even erased—then we can adhere to a simulation of what we might be(come). The object of inquiry has disappeared: "When the real is no longer what it used to be, nostalgia assumes its full meaning" (Baudrillard, 1983, p. 12). In my experience teaching, students often have been led to believe that everything is gradually getting better: we may have problems now but look how much progress we have made! Although perhaps well-intentioned, such framings can be very harmful. With just a drive for progress, we might be tempted to make a lesson out of others' pain—their suffering served the purpose of teaching us what (not) to do. In this way, we might feel comforted that horrors such as genocide have served a higher purpose, instead of grappling with the fact that they ought to not have happened, and no justification exists. Furthermore, without a referent to *Evils* and evils in the past, there is a danger to suppress those in the present. Furthermore, those who consider themselves to be "good" fail to see any ambivalence or blurring; rather, they create an "illusory identity" based on minimizing or eliminating misfortunes such as poverty, violence, and death (Pawlett, 2007, p. 129). We identify ourselves as good people if we help simply soften current miseries instead of seeking to create something new by thinking radically.

Attempts to Control the Unpleasant

As an example, how individuals and societies manage poverty illustrates how we mismanage *Evil*. The relative nature of poverty not only functions to help further the blurring but by its very nature creates a competition for who can be the most good, not in the altruistic sense of the word but rather as the inverse of suffering. Individuals and groups will fundraise to "eliminate" poverty, but with the emphasis on their own "good" actions in social comparison with others (e.g., I donated this much to charity, what have you done?). Yet, the economic structure of many countries creates the underlying disparity (after all, where there is profit there must somewhere else be a deficit).

When the unequal origin of current economic systems is glossed over in favour of a narrative of progress, the solutions to the supposed problem, then, are superficial—treating the symptoms (e.g., lack of food, housing) instead of the disease (inequality). *Evil* could help societies fight the evil/misfortune of poverty, as there is an opportunity for thinking and acting upon radical solutions to the root problem. First, there needs to be a new narrative, one that is not of sanitized progress, and then individuals and societies and those living within them need to consider the yet unknown, being open to trying what has not yet been tried. But, so long as *Evil* is denied as a potential creative force, it is relegated to the sidelines with the hopes of obliteration.

Even if we are relatively successful in removing all misfortune from our lives, we can cause it to reappear and fracture happiness, "making it unbearable, diverting happiness and misfortune into despair—the despair of having everything and nothing" (Pawlett, 2014, §5, para. 2). Some maintain that death is required for life to have meaning (e.g., Frankl, 1986; Williams, 1973), and perhaps similarly *Evil* and even evil/misfortune is needed to give happiness meaning: "there is nowhere a definition of Good or for anyone a clear definition of happiness" (Baudrillard, 2004/2005, p. 154). Without *Evil* and misfortune, happiness would become a strictly functional existence that is devoid of the drive for salvation that provides meaning to our actions.

CREATIVE ENERGY

Evil can be seen positively in great revolutionaries who tap into it as "the energy of challenge, defiance, creativity, and renewal" (Pawlett, 2014, §3, para. 1). We need *Symbolic Evil* to avoid stagnation—and in education, this could not be needed more. To rise above bureaucratic authority, it requires *Evil*'s creative energy for defiance and renewal, and yet the system does everything in its power to eliminate it: "The great religious and political revolutionaries (Jesus, Che Guevara, Nelson Mandela) are clearly 'Evil' from the perspective of the system of law and order they challenge, and they are punished accordingly" (Pawlett, 2014, §3, para. 1).

When the curriculum calls for discussions of those who have been part of revolutions, Baudrillard's understanding of *Evil* can be a productive tool for critical thinking. How were these individuals and the groups they were part of create something new? How might we judge these as helpful or harmful? To what extent might we see (or not see) similar processes in play during our lifetimes? In addition to Guevara and Mandela mentioned above, examples could include: Maximilien Robespierre from the French Revolution (particularly during the Reign of Terror); Vladimir Lenin from the Bolshevik Revolution; Mohandas Gandhi from the Indian independence movement; Muammar Al Gaddafi's revolution in Libya; Simon Bolivar's decolonial work in Peru, Bolivar, Colombia, Ecuador, and Venezuela; Martin Luther from the Protestant Reformation; Malcolm X's actions during the civil rights movement in the United States; and Kathleen Neal Cleaver's work as a member of the Black Panther Party.

Historical examples are insufficient on their own. There are countless examples to be found, but teachers need to consider engaging with recent examples that students might relate to, for example, Asmaa Mahfouz. She is a contemporary revolutionary who is credited with sparking the January 2011 uprising in Egypt through a video blog post encouraging others to join her in protest in Tahrir Square. She is considered one of the leaders of the Egyptian Revolution and is a prominent member of Egypt's Coalition of the Youth of the Revolution. A recent example has the advantage (hopefully) of students realizing that the process of *Evil* is ongoing—not static in the past.

Baudrillard's framing of great revolutionaries tends to focus on the individual, which ignores the milieu and communities which support the rise of these particular figures in historical and contemporary times. This situation runs the risk of robbing students of their sense of agency as part of inherently interconnected movements (e.g., Woodson, 2016). Conversely, when a revolution occurs and ends badly, we might blame that individual and ignore the culpability of others, or even ourselves, and thus also disempowering us (van Kessel & Crowley, 2017). For a more thorough discussion of this phenomenon, see Chapter 3, but for our purposes here (i.e., teaching revolutionaries in the context of *Symbolic Evil*), there is a call for teachers to be attentive to the milieu as much as the individual.

Regardless of the example(s) engaged with, it is important to note that while these revolutionaries were taking action, it is difficult, if not impossible, to know whether these revolutions would lead to something helpful or harmful. We know now that Robespierre and his Reign of Terror resulted in much unnecessary bloodshed and cruelty—now that we have the benefit of hindsight. Libya's revolution under Gaddafi seemed quite good at the time—a bloodless coup even—but in more recent history we tend to judge him as despotic. Malcolm X, at the time, was not seen as a positive force for change, but with the benefit of hindsight, we know that he made a massive difference in the civil rights movement. *Symbolic Evil* is a force of change, and so it is impossible to determine its degree of helpfulness at the time.

An Education System for *Evil*

Evil can also be discussed beyond curriculum—at the level of the schooling system. What might happen if schools engaged with *Symbolic Evil*? Classrooms, curriculum, and assessment would all look radically different, and such changes cannot be the result of minor tweaks. Real change—significant and worthy change—needs to happen at the ideological level. *Symbolic Evil* provides an intellectual framing to encourage radical change without being prescriptive. Societies vary from each other, and even the same society can vary greatly over time, so there is no simple answer to the question of how we might live together. Arguably, the danger lies with stagnation and limits placed upon creative energies. We can, however, begin from a point of what might need to change.

Student "Success"

To begin, I feel that we need to examine the broader question of what we want student "success" to look like. How do we define success? At first, this question seems easy. It is assumed that we want students to gain future employment and thus schools are to develop the knowledge, skills, and attitudes that will help them obtain those jobs. Success, then, is tied to the completion of requirements, such as standardized tests and a high school diploma. Education as a system in this case is expected to have the foresight to predict those future employment possibilities that its standardized tests are being used to screen for, an expectation that is intrinsically flawed. When success is the equivalent to test scores, the argument then develops regarding what sort of curriculum best meets that goal, at times pitting one subject area against another based on perceived, but not defined, future needs (e.g., mathematics and the sciences over the humanities and the arts). This situation is exacerbated by generalized economic fears. We worry that a lack of success for individual students is tied to eventual economic failure, largely in terms of future employability, as well as a loss of revenue and prestige for both students and institutions (Archer, Chetty, & Prinsloo, 2014). In educational research, scholars have made clear the link between disengagement (and lack of "success") and unemployment after leaving compulsory school. This issue is often framed in terms of its cost to society (e.g., Pacheco & Dye, 2013). DeLuca et al. (2010) researched disengaged, at-risk youth fresh into the workplace and their experiences. The justification for this research is rooted in the fear of "a growing youth employment crisis" and its potentially disastrous implications for even strong economies like Canada's (DeLuca et al., 2010, p. 305). This study and others like it (e.g., DeLuca, Godden, Hutchinson, & Versnel, 2015) have called for increased vocational (work-based) schooling.

What might happen, however, when we begin to look into this notion of purely economic success a little further? We might ask ourselves different questions. What sort of employment is deemed desirable? What does employment accomplish? Is there more to success than accumulating money and possessions? If yes, what might that success look like? These questions are being asked today by groups such as the New Economics Foundation (NEF) which has created the "Happy Planet Index" that measures the extent to which "countries deliver long, happy, sustainable lives... [using] global data on life expectancy, experienced well-being and ecological footprint" (New Economics Foundation [NEF], 2014). Despite Baudrillard's scepticism about our capacity to define happiness, measuring and valuing happiness is not a recent phenomenon, although it is not common. The Fourth King of Bhutan, King Jigme Singye Wangchuck, declared in 1972 that "Gross National Happiness is more important than Gross Domestic Product" (Oxford Poverty & Human Development Initiative [OPHI], n.d., para. 1). The criteria for this measure consist of: living standards, health, education, good governance, ecological diversity and resilience, time use, psychological well-being, cultural diversity and resilience, and community vitality (Centre for Bhutan Studies & GNH Research, 2016). Such an emphasis on the conditions for happiness impacts social and political policy in a different way than a purely economic focus would.

Corporations, Jobs, and Schooling

An obstacle to redefining success is the false assumption that as a society we are bound to a balanced budget regardless of the human, animal, or environmental cost, as is the aim of neoliberalism (Abdi & Ellis, 2007, p. 289). Although liberalism in its variety of forms has only existed for a small fraction of human history, its values underpin our society often seemingly without question. There is a false assumption that "capitalism just goes on and on, getting worse or better depending on one's point of view" (Wark, 2014, para. 4). Neoliberalism has expanded beyond policies to a form of social rule that influences such things as speculative capital, reductions in social development programs, deregulating and reducing taxes for corporations, and of course excessive consumerism. When money and its associated prestige are the priorities, automatically our possible conceptions of success are narrowed.

118   C. van KESSEL

In Canada and elsewhere, corporations maintain society, including education. In particular, the brand-name value of a company has had an impact on education, as there have been fears that education is suffering as institutional priorities shift "to those programs most conducive to private sector partnership" (Klein, 2000, p. xviii). Such fears were exacerbated in Alberta during the recent push for curriculum redesign with the inclusion of oil and gas companies as part of an advisory committee, particularly for early elementary curriculum. This corporate inclusion inspired an uproar leading to such actions as a petition with over 26,000 signatures (Smith, 2014, p. 30). Support for corporate advice likely stems from the belief that we must prepare them for contemporary jobs in Alberta. Job preparation, however, can only be classified as *schooling* but not *education*. Stemming from the Latin verb, *educāre*, education is more than training; it is synonymous with rearing a child. We expect parents to provide more than an economic foundation, and we should expect that for schools as well. Instead of a factory model of producing thoughtless consumers, schools might educate to helpful relations with each other and the planet.

So what might the purpose of schools be, if it is not solely for jobs? According to Gert Biesta (2010), schools are generally thought to address three distinct but interrelated functions or aims:

1. "qualification" for public–private competency, including specific training for a particular skill or job to more generalized preparation such as life skills or political and cultural literacy.
2. "socialization" to initiate students into society, ranging from ways of speaking and comportment to disciplinary "ways of knowing" (e.g., thinking like an historian or scientist).
3. "subjectification" to facilitate students developing their own way of being; e.g., thought and action potentially independent from the present way of doing so.

Through the lens of Baudrillard, part of subjectification would include encouraging students (and ourselves) to tap into *Symbolic Evil*. Subjectification—the process of being a subject (as in being the subject of a sentence who actively *does* something)—can involve new ways of thinking and being in the world. Although I doubt any parent wants their child to grow up deficient in any one of those three aims (qualification, socialization, and subjectification), an overemphasis on qualification and socialization at the cost of subjectification and *Symbolic Evil* fails to develop human beings capable of independent thought and action, meanwhile trapping us in an out-dated ideology that has failed humans and the planet alike. There is no standardized test for subjectification, and thus for meaningful change to happen, the system must be over-hauled, not tweaked. This shift would change how we see employment, as something that is valued more for helping obtain harmony rather than a financial endgame. Success in this model has less to do with money and jobs and more to do with happiness for humans and other living and non-living entities on this planet. This model affords us an opportunity to make radical breaks with the present system—instead of mimicking the consumerist patterns we have inherited; there is the support for thinking in new ways.

Classroom Climate

In terms of classroom environments themselves, it is easy to react severely to disruptions that challenge the status quo. From my own experiences as a teacher of classes with high-stakes testing for university entrance, students who refuse to engage in the process can be frustrating for both personal and professional reasons. When certain students see through the transparency of the educational structure, when they see how standardized tests largely test one's ability to take that test instead of real learning, perhaps we might approach them with the attitude that they may be seeking *Evil* and its radical break with the status quo instead of seeing them as an obstacle to a test result. Baudrillard's conceptualization of *Evil* provides educators with an opportunity to rethink how we deal with youth disengagement. The *Evil* that diverts and reverses has revealed that we might be doing youth a disservice by assuming that their lack of enthusiasm for school is their own personal failing.

Based on Pinar (2009), classroom teachers can acknowledge the dominant situation and then intervene to provide space for students to examine how culture is transmitted and the ways we might subvert the passive duplication of undesirable explicit and implicit curriculum and pedagogy. What Baudrillard's philosophy adds to the discussion is a provocation about how radical change can happen. Engaging with the creativity of *Symbolic Evil* can provide the space for something new to emerge—a new way of thinking or doing, both of which require teachers to assume guilt not on the part of the individual or groups in society, but rather flaws with society itself. The trick is, of course, how to create such a space, especially given that there can be no formula for success, no one correct answer. Much educational discourse focuses on universalizing best practices—not promoting the emergence of the unknown. This situation is understandable, given that embracing the uncertainty and possibility of *Evil* is a frightening proposition. Troubling our taken-for-granted false sense of reality is a first step and can be accomplished in countless ways.

FATAL STRATEGIES

Teachers can undergo their own processes of *Evil*, and they can support students in this endeavour as well. Radical thinking in students is to be encouraged, rather than seen as threatening. Resistance, however, is easily incorporated and assimilated back into the dominant structure, and so attempts at encouraging creative and radical thought cannot merely be part of the curriculum, or in any other way forced or scripted. Critical theory has (rightly so) critiqued violent power structures, including taken-for-granted norms. Fatal theory, drawing form *Symbolic Evil*, does the same, but the form of the strategy is as important as the critique itself (i.e., the how as well as the what). Critical theory can often fall into unhelpful strategies like snark, which the existence system can render impotent:

> Snide remarks or "snark" as a reaction to offensive or anti-progressive rhetoric and policy has become an increasingly popular means of garnering online attention through displays of cleverness... snark falls into the category of a form of resistance or critique that gets absorbed into the code. (Kline, 2016, p. 110)

When I read Kline's (2016) comments, I think of the character of Mr. Smith from *The Matrix* (Wachowski & Wachowski, 1999). As an evolving computer program, Mr. Smith absorbs anything the humans develop to resist him and then uses that against the humans. In real life, we see such absorption all the time, for example you can buy anarchist t-shirts at the mall. Critiques of the system can all too easily become part of that system. Fatal strategies and *Symbolic Evil* do not provide a simple method of subversion, perhaps frustrating so, and yet this tension is fundamental to the theory itself:

> it is important to admit that this application work [of fatal theory] will not result in any policy or practice suggestions. Such is not the outcome of the pursuit of fatal strategies and its accompanying radical thought. Rather,

their aim is well beyond the level of policy as they seek to push on the negative conditions of the system until it reverses course. Radical thought can be accompanied by what Baudrillard terms "theory fiction" as a way of rendering the world enigmatic, as a means of staying at the margins in order to anticipate the world and its events that he claimed critical thought was lagging behind. (Kline, 2016, p. 111)

As such, the call for *Evil* in education is more of a sensibility than a method, a call to push back against stagnant, harmful systems and valuing radical ideas more so than what would "work" within the existing system. By destabilizing existing structures, there lies an opportunity for change. Although impossible to determine in advance if a dramatic reimagining will end well for us, that is a risk worth taking.

REFERENCES

Abdi, A. A., & Ellis, L. (2007). Education and Zambia's democratic development: Reconstructing "something" from the predatory project of neoliberal globalization. *Alberta Journal of Educational Research, 53*(3), 287–301.

Archer, E., Chetty, Y. B., & Prinsloo, P. (2014). Benchmarking the habits and behaviours of successful students: A case study of academic-business collaboration. *International Review of Research in Open and Distance Learning, 15*(1), 62–83.

Bataille, G. (1988). *The accursed share: An essay on general economy.* New York, NY: Zone Books. (Original work published in 1949)

Baudrillard, J. (1983). *Simulations* (P. Foss, P. Patton, & P. Beitchman, Trans.). New York, NY: Semiotext(e).

Baudrillard, J. (1993). *The transparency of evil* (J. Benedict, Trans.). London, UK: Verso. (Original work published in 1990)

Baudrillard, J. (1998). When Bataille attacked the metaphysical principle of economy. In F. Botting & S. Wilson (Eds.), *Bataille: A critical reader* (pp. 191–195). Malden, MA: Blackwell.

Baudrillard, J. (2005). *The intelligence of evil or the lucidity pact* (C. Turner, Trans.). Oxford, UK: Berg. (Original work published in 2004)

Biesta, G. (2010). *Good education in an age of measurement: Ethics, politics, democracy.* Boulder, CO: Paradigm.

Boldt-Irons, L. (2001). Bataille and Baudrillard: From a general economy to the transparency of evil. *Angelaki, 6*(2), 79–89.

Centre for Bhutan Studies & GNH Research. (2016). *A compass towards a just and harmonious society: 2015 GNH Survey Report.* Thimphu, Bhutan: Centre for Bhutan Studies & GNH Research. Retrieved from http://www.

grossnationalhappiness.com/wp-content/uploads/2017/01/Final-GNH-Report-jp-21.3.17-ilovepdf-compressed.pdf.

DeLuca, C., Godden, L., Hutchinson, N. L., & Versnel, J. (2015). Preparing at-risk youth for a changing world: Revisiting a person-in-context model for transition to employment. *Educational Research, 57*(2), 182–200.

DeLuca, C., Hutchinson, N. L, deLugt, J. S., Beyer, W., Thornton, A., Versnel, J., ... Munby, H. (2010). Learning in the workplace: Fostering resilience in disengaged youth. *Work, 36*, 305–319.

Frankl, V. (1986). *The doctor and the soul* (R. Winston & C. Winston, Trans.). New York, NY: Vintage.

Kant, I. (1838). *Religion within the boundary of pure reason* (J. W. Semple, Trans.). Edinburgh, Scotland: Thomas Clark. (Original work published in 1793)

Klein, N. (2000). *No logo: Taking aim at the brand bullies.* Toronto, ON: Vintage.

Kline, K. (2016). *Baudrillard, youth, and American film.* Lanham, MD: Lexington.

Livni, E. (2018, September 16). Everyone hates postmodernism—But that doesn't make it wrong. *Quartz.* Retrieved from https://qz.com/1388555/everyone-hates-postmodernism-but-that-doesnt-make-it-false/.

Merrin, W. (2007, March 8). Jean Baudrillard: 1929–2007. *Evatt Foundation.* Retrieved from http://evatt.org.au/news/jean-baudrillard-1929-2007.html.

New Economics Foundation. (2014). *About the happy planet index.* Retrieved from http://www.happyplanetindex.org/about/.

Oxford Poverty & Human Development Initiative (OPHI). (n.d.). Bhutan's gross national happiness index. *OPHI.* Retrieved from https://ophi.org.uk/policy/national-policy/gross-national-happiness-index/.

Pacheco, G., & Dye, J. (2013). Estimating the cost of youth disengagement in New Zealand. *New Zealand Journal of Employment Relations, 38*(2), 47–63.

Pawlett, W. (2007). *Jean Baudrillard: Against banality.* London, UK: Routledge.

Pawlett, W. (2014). Baudrillard's duality: Manichaeism and the principle of evil. *International Journal of Baudrillard Studies, 11*(1). Retrieved from http://www2.ubishops.ca/baudrillardstudies/vol11_1/v11-1-pawlett.html.

Pinar, W. F. (2009). *The worldliness of a cosmopolitan education.* New York, NY: Routledge.

Smith, J. (2014). Overhauling everything schools teach kids. *Albertaviews, 17*(7), 30–34.

van Kessel, C. (2016). The transparency of evil in *The Leftovers* and its implications for student (dis)engagement. *Educational Studies, 52*(1), 51–67. https://doi.org/10.1080/00131946.2015.1120206.

van Kessel, C., & Crowley, R. M. (2017). Villainification and evil in social studies education. *Theory & Research in Social Education, 95*, 427–455. https://doi.org/10.1080/00933104.2017.1285734.

van Kessel, C., & Kline, K. (2019). "If you can't tell, does it matter?": *Westworld, the murder of the real, and 21st century schooling. Journal of Curriculum and Pedagogy*. Advance online publication. https://doi.org/10.1080/15505 170.2018.1542358.

Wachowski, L., & Wachowski, L. (Directors) (1999). *The matrix* [motion picture]. Burbank, CA: Warner.

Wark, M. (2014, April 30). Is this still capitalism? *Public Seminar Commons, 1*(2). Retrieved from http://www.publicseminar.org/2014/04/is-this-still-capitalism/#.VBUFly5dWMV.

Williams, B. (1973). The Makropulos case: Reflections on the tedium of immortality. In B. Williams (Ed.), *Problems of the self* (pp. 82–100). Cambridge: Cambridge University Press.

Woodson, A. N. (2016). We're just ordinary people: Messianic master narratives and Black youths' civic agency. *Theory & Research in Social Education, 44,* 184–211.

CHAPTER 7

Evil, Existential Terror, and Classroom Climate

Ernest Becker noted that, ironically, the worst evils are created in the process of us trying to escape from evil. Humans commit terrible acts that arise from our fight against the evil of death. This chapter discusses how aspects of our curriculum and pedagogy are shaped by attempts to escape anxiety about our own mortality. There is a particular focus on the profession of teaching as an immortality project (potentially helpful and harmful), as well as how we encounter resistance to alternative viewpoints arising from worldview threat.

ERNEST BECKER

Ernest Becker was a Jewish-American cultural anthropologist. He served in the U.S. infantry in the Second World War, and his unit helped liberate a Nazi concentration camp. After working for a time at the U.S. Embassy in Paris, he pursued graduate studies and then taught at a variety of institutions, ending his career at Simon Fraser University in Canada before his death due to colon cancer at the age of 49. Becker's series of often non-continuous, one-year appointments can be partly attributed to the controversial stances he took supporting academic freedom and the civil rights movement, and opposing the Vietnam War and "authoritarian educational practices," especially "the dangers to academic independence and freedom posed by the common practice of the universities to seek and rely on military and business sources for research contracts" (Liechty, 2015, para. 8).

© The Author(s) 2019
C. van Kessel, *An Education in 'Evil'*,
Palgrave Studies in Educational Futures,
https://doi.org/10.1007/978-3-030-16605-2_7

125

In his Pulitzer Prize-winning book, *The Denial of Death* (1973), he began with how the end of our lives shapes what happens before it:

> the idea of death, the fear of it, haunts the human animal like nothing else; it is a mainspring of human activity—activity designed largely to avoid the fatality of death, to overcome it by denying in some way that it is the final destiny for man [sic]. (p. xvii)

Although Becker's work is peppered with the questionable language and phrasing of his time (e.g., gender exclusive language such as "man," and troubling, value-laden vocabulary like "primitive"), the ideas of commitments in his work can operate in helpful ways. Feminist lenses have brought new relevancy to Becker as he provides insight into the existential motivation that drives the patriarchy (e.g., Heflick, Goldenberg, Cooper, & Puvia, 2011; Roberts, Goldenberg, Power, & Pyszczynski, 2002). I believe that decolonial lenses could function similarly in relation to his work.

Becker was drawn to a multiplicity of intellectual approaches. His PhD dissertation was on Zen Buddhism, and during that process, he moved beyond just anthropology and discovered psychoanalysis. Such a cross-disciplinary approach shaped his future academic pursuits, as Becker understood that big questions cannot be answered by a single discipline (and certainly not one particular theorist within any one discipline). Thus, Becker turned to many different thinkers and fields. To name a few, Becker drew from: psychologists and psychoanalysts such as Sigmund Freud, Erich Fromm, and Otto Rank; philosophers like Søren Kierkegaard, Norman O. Brown, and Paul Tillich; anthropologists like A. M. Hocart; and naturalists like Charles Darwin. Becker engaged with ideas about symbolic existence, human evil, dread, and, perhaps most importantly, that the fear of death is a fundamental aspect of human motivation.

Frightened to Death

Human motivation is multifaceted and layered, and yet death is, in many ways, the worm at the core of existence (Solomon, Greenberg, & Pyszczynski, 2015). Our fear of death influences human behaviour in fascinating ways. Some of these ways are logical, such as how we might seek to extend our lives literally (e.g., life-extending practices or procedures) or symbolically (e.g., through leaving a mark on the world). Other effects are more surprising, such as how we relate to individuals and groups who have different worldviews. If humans were to experience unmitigated existential fear it would interfere with many effective forms of thought and action. As such, we have developed a defensive psychological system geared towards keeping thoughts of human mortality away from our consciousness, thus limiting the potential for debilitating anxiety. The principal way humans manage the fear of death is through the construction and maintenance of cultural worldviews and self-esteem.

Before delving too far into how humans compensate for our existential fear, it is first important to consider how humans come to be into that state in the first place. At the heart of Becker's work is the assumption that human brains have an evolved complexity which has provided us with survival advantages, including anticipating future outcomes, planning, cooperating, and overcoming environmental challenges. This awareness of ourselves in the world around us, however, is a double-edged sword. Because we have the capacity to imagine our futures, we also understand that we are subject to the same natural processes as other animals—specifically aeging, decay, and ultimately death. It is possible that other animals have a similar knowledge of their eventual demise, but because our communication with other animals is limited, it is currently impossible to tell. It is, however, safe to say that humans are keenly aware. In fact, it is difficult to imagine a situation where we are ignorant of our impending doom, and yet it is an interesting thought experiment:

> Let's suppose, contrary to the way things really are, that death was something of which we were unaware until it happened. It would be as though death were a bolt from the blue. We lived our lives, engaged in our various commitments and involvements, and then one day we just stopped living. It's a difficult world to imagine, since we would have to account for how we notice other people no longer living without our wondering what that might have to do with us. But let's suppose we could do it. Would that change anything about the role death plays in our lives? If we had no awareness of it, would it remain the most important fact about us? (May, 2009, p. 6)

Judging from Ernest Becker's work, death would not play as large of a role. Humans seek to compensate for their impermanence, seeking

128   C. van KESSEL

immortality to thwart our fleeting existence. The hypothetical situation Todd May (2009) spoke of—thinking we are immortal even though we were not—would shape our lives differently: How we interact with each other, especially, as well as our desires (or perhaps, then, a lack thereof) to leave our mark on the world. What "makes a life meaningful or worthwhile" might change (May, 2009, p. 10). Like all other organisms, we desire to keep on living, and so the knowledge of inevitable mortality can be intensely troubling, and yet it is, as May (2009) aptly noted, "the fact that we die is the most important fact about us" (p. 4).

Terror Management Theory

Jeff Greenberg, Tom Pyszczynski, and Sheldon Solomon (1986) developed terror management theory (TMT) to test Becker's ideas, and in over thirty years, there have been hundreds of TMT experiments that span multiple cultural and geographic contexts. TMT addresses how humans (don't) deal with death:

> According to the theory, the problem of death resides beneath consciousness and, from there, triggers distal death defenses—the maintenance of worldviews and self-esteem. The conscious contemplation of death is defended against differently according to TMT; it is dealt with more rationally by denying vulnerability to physical death or pushing it into the distant future using proximal death defenses such as a conscious thought about one's excellent state of physical health or one's family trend toward longevity. (Burke, Martens, & Faucher, 2010, p. 156; see also Pyszczynski, Greenberg, & Solomon, 1999)

In the realm of experimental social psychology, TMT researchers have developed hypotheses to determine how our fear of death shapes how we carry out our lives. Two main hypotheses emerged: the *mortality salience hypothesis* and the *death-thought accessibility hypothesis* (for a more robust presentation of supporting TMT literature, see Schimel, Hayes, & Sharp, 2018).

The mortality salience (MS) hypothesis posits that reminding people of death temporarily increases their need for protective psychological structures, such as staunch adherence to a cultural worldview. MS manipulations usually involve priming participants with either the idea of death or a control topic, and then observing the effects in a specific context.

These death primes can be very direct (e.g., considering death overtly, such as answering essay questions about death) or more indirect (e.g., interviewing participants near a funeral home or subliminally flashing the word "death" across a computer screen). Control groups are often used to differentiate existential fear from other sources of anxiety or discomfort (e.g., writing or reading about dental pain). A meta-analysis of 164 empirical studies with 277 experiments has shown that the MS hypothesis is a strong one: "The magnitude for the effect was $r=.35$, which attained the top quartile of effects for psychology in general and the 80th percentile for theories in personality and social psychology" (Burke et al., 2010, p. 185). In less technical terms, this statement means that TMT experiments show a linear relationship regarding the effects of MS (i.e., the hypothesis is sound according to the standards of the academic field).

Although there are many beautiful gifts that the knowledge of our mortality can inspire (even just by simply providing us with direction during our lives), not all of our defences against death are helpful. The MS hypothesis predicts that humans will adhere more excessively and rigidly to their worldviews if they are reminded of death. One of the first studies that tested this hypothesis was done with municipal court judges in the city of Tucson, Arizona (Rosenblatt, Greenberg, Solomon, Pyszczynski, & Lyon, 1989). Judges reviewed a case brief for a prostitution charge, with those in the experimental group being made aware of their own mortality, and then they suggested a bond amount for the accused. It is fair to assume that upholding the law is a central component of a judge's worldview, and therefore, per the MS hypothesis, judges who were reminded of death should defend their worldview by reacting more harshly towards those that break the law—in this situation, suggesting a higher amount than those not prompted to think about death. Control group judges who did not complete the exercise (where they were asked to reflect and write about their own death) suggested an average bond of $50, which aligned with standard practice. Judges in the MS condition suggested an outrageous average bond of $455. Support for the MS hypothesis has been obtained cross-culturally, that is, reminders of death have produced effects on worldview defence in divergent contexts (e.g., Canada, China, Germany, India, Iran, Italy, Israel, Japan, United States). Moreover, substantial bodies of evidence have found these effects to be specific to heightened accessibility of death-related thought and different from the effects of thinking of other aversive topics (e.g., uncertainty, social exclusion, intense physical pain, or a looming exam).

130   C. van KESSEL

The death-thought accessibility (DTA) hypothesis predicts that if cultural worldviews function to buffer individuals from thoughts of death, then threatening or weakening these psychological structures should increase the accessibility of death-thoughts. DTA is typically measured using a word-fragment completion task in which participants are asked to complete each fragment in succession with the first word that comes to mind. Some words in the list can be completed as either a death-related word or a non-death-related word. For example, the fragment, "S K _ L L" could be completed as "SKULL" or "SKILL." The more death words people complete, the more it can be inferred that death thoughts are close to consciousness (for an example of a DTA measure, see the appendix of Webber, Zhang, Schimel, & Blatter, 2016). The first set of studies testing the DTA hypothesis with respect to cultural worldviews was conducted among Canadian participants (Schimel, Hayes, Williams, & Jahrig, 2007). Participants viewed a web page that belittled an array of Canadian cultural values and achievements (e.g., diet, love of hockey, universal healthcare, being polite), whereas in the control condition participants viewed a parallel web page that derogated Australian culture. The results consistently showed higher levels of DTA in the anti-Canada (worldview threat) condition compared to the anti-Australia (control) condition. These results were not due to an overall increase in negative thoughts or anger but appeared to be specifically due to the worldview threatening nature of the web page.

TMT, through the MS and DTA hypotheses, identify how thoughts and fears of death beneath our consciousness shape our behaviour. Humans need to compensate for our impermanence. What does this existential situation mean for teaching? Of the many immortality projects, we might have, teaching can be an effective one, especially given the potential impact teachers can have on their students (for better or for worse). Furthermore, TMT provides an explanation for why dialoguing across divergent viewpoints is so difficult in classrooms (and beyond).

TEACHING AS AN IMMORTALITY PROJECT

Ultimately, self-esteem and maintaining one's faith in a cultural worldview serve to alleviate the fear of inevitable death by providing a sense of life-continuity or immortality, which can function literally or symbolically. The TMT sense of *self-esteem* (not to be confused with a more commonplace understanding of the term) does not have the endgame of simply bolstering self-confidence; rather, it is specifically the feelings of having a meaningful, significant existence. This self-esteem is linked to our literal and symbolic immortality. Literal immortality refers to the story a culture tells the group about what happens after death, which for most of the world's religions involves some form of an afterlife. There are non-religious understandings as well, such as taking comfort in the recycling of the atoms and energy that make up our bodies per the First Law of Thermodynamics. Symbolic immortality refers to symbolic extensions of the self through lifelong achievements (e.g., books, works of art, children) that will live on in the culture after physical death. May (2009) described how such immortality projects can function:

> How does this assurance work? It is obviously of no use to one after one has died. If I have a building erected in my name, I will not know about this building after my death. It will give me no solace then. It can operate only as an assurance for the living. I donate money for a building that will bear my name, telling myself that after I die I will be remembered. And in that memory I will live on. This does not have to be my only motive for donating money for a building. For those who donate—or write books, or have children—it may not be a motive at all. But for those for whom it is a motive, it probably works as a consolation to the living while they are alive. (p. 84)

Although literally we still perish, symbolically we live on—small consolation, but effective psychologically (Solomon et al., 2015).

The pursuit of self-esteem through teaching can be considered a symbolic immortality project when the terror of individual death is alleviated by the teacher's ability to pass along particular values and attitudes to their students; i.e., teachers can reproduce certain versions of themselves through schooling (van Kessel & Burke, 2018). Along this line, teachers can see their students similarly to how they might see their children. Teachers-as-quasi-parents can bequeath their ideas and commitments as part of their legacy to the next generation. The profession has long been fundamentally about creating legacies, illustrated by the common practice of teachers referring to their students as their own: "my kids" or "our kids" (e.g., Clandinin & Connelly, 1996, p. 28; Howard & Johnson, 2004, p. 16). Studies have shown that reminders of mortality increase the desire for offspring (Fritsche et al., 2007), and perhaps this translates to teachers desiring a certain form of emulation by their students (although this hypothesis is yet to be tested).

132 C. van KESSEL

Teaching has been linked to the sort of vicarious immortality that Becker describes (Bailey, 1946; Bregman, 1985; Ciaccio, 2000; Roberts, 2008). Indeed, Butterfield (1921) described that:

> The teacher rejoices that the truth that he teaches will become part of the life of the generation which follows and so as a torch of light will be passed on while civilization remains. Of all the great professions and the common occupations, teaching is most to be desired, since it most completely satisfies the human yearning for extended mortality. (p. 289)

For some, teaching as an immortality project is an ideal, so long as teachers refrain from indulging in narcissism. Blacker (1997) identified a Socratic "search for the cosmos, for the truth about the universe, not because it creates for oneself new and fashionable -isms or a circle of devotees" (p. 8), and somewhat similarly Dahlbeck (2015) noted a Spinozistic teacher as "geared to guiding students toward a more rational life, at the same time as it is geared to the self-improvement of the teacher" (p. 357). For Blacker (1997) and Dahlbeck (2015), its problem is not the quasi-immortality gained through the practice of teaching in and of itself; rather, it is the degree of self-indulgence as part of that situation. Yet, it is vital for us to question the goal of recreating the self in education. This framing is not to downplay that teachers can make a difference in the students' lives; rather, the call is to be thoughtful about our motivations and the potential harmful (albeit unintended) consequences.

With teaching as an immortality project, both students' and teachers' lives are on the line. Because teaching is at least partly about delaying the terror of individual death, there is a danger of overinvestment in moulding students in a very particular way, thus foreclosing educational opportunities. Gert Biesta (e.g., 2010) has noted the difference between *education* and *schooling*—with schooling being more about qualification and socialization, and education involving subjectification (i.e., the process of becoming a subject, thinking independently from authority and yet interconnected with others). If we pursue, consciously or unconsciously, the reproduction of ourselves, then there are limited possibilities for subjectification. Students are tasked with parroting our own commitments and claims to knowledge. W. B. Yeats is attributed with the saying: "Education is not the filling of a pail, but the lighting of a fire," a saying for which there does not seem to be a source, and is similar to Plutarch's statement: "For the mind does not require filling like a bottle, but rather, like wood, it only requires kindling to create in it an impulse to think independently and an ardent desire for the truth" (1927, pp. 258–259). Regardless of attribution, subjectification, like fire, can be instigated, but not controlled. As professionals, teachers can and should carefully select a variety of wood species (i.e., specifics of curriculum) and methods of igniting them (i.e., pedagogical techniques), and play with them in various combinations to see the different fires that might be sparked in students. This attitude towards education stands in stark opposition with the sort of teaching where the students must simply mimic their instructor.

It would be unfair to paint teachers undertaking in an immortality project as purely selfish. In my own observations, there is often a robust, even laudable, commitment that underlies a desire for the world to be a better place, and for students to be successful and happy. The danger lies in failing to listen to our students and their particular needs and desires. Within teaching is a semblance of a saviour-complex (Burke & Segall, 2015) with the explicit goal "to make a difference in the lives of students" (Fullan, 1993, p. 1), but as Freire (1989) aptly noted, there is a danger of acting *for* the oppressed instead of *with* them. To be clear, I think that all people, including teachers, should do whatever they can to work towards their preferred future for society, but it is folly to place expectations on an individual teacher to change the world singlehandedly. Teachers need to consider what their theory of change is—the mechanisms by which societies have transformed and will continue to—and then operate within that framework.

The immortal teacher is an individual, and this framing alone is potentially damaging. Drawing from her work with preservice teachers in secondary education, Deborah P. Britzman (1986) identified three cultural myths: everything depends on the teacher, the teacher is the expert, and teachers are self-made. Rooted in the rampant beliefs in a sort of "rugged" individualism (Britzman, 1986, p. 442), these beliefs can isolate a teacher and prevent them from working effectively towards preferred futures; for example, assuming one needs to be an expert might contribute to the excuse of "cultural disqualification" that prevents educational engagements with Indigenous perspectives (Donald, 2009). If teachers are considered to be "a unitary and expert source and master of knowledge" then teacher candidates "will never know enough about how to teach and about teaching materials to in fact 'teach'" (Madden, 2016, p. 49).

134   C. van KESSEL

Furthermore, there is a danger to psychological well-being when teachers' professional self-esteem and status as immortal are contingent upon students mimicking their beliefs and actions. If teachers do not receive the attention from their students and colleagues as expected, if students do not carry on the values, skills, etc. of their teacher, the teacher is denied their symbolic immortality. Without another source of existential comfort, the teacher is left to confront their impermanence, and perhaps feel insignificant. Creating legacies helps teachers deal with death, even if they are not aware of this motivating force, but the cost is that we create a situation with cosmic stakes. Although teachers can begin their careers brimming with a moral purpose that is construed as socially meaningful, they can burn out and sink into despair with a growing "sense of inconsequentiality" (Farber, 1991, p. 36). We need to challenge the teacher-as-saviour model, which involves interrogating the existential elements that underlie it.

RESISTANCES TO DIVERGENT VIEWPOINTS

As Becker (1973) stated, our cultural worldview "is more than merely an outlook on life: it is an immortality formula" (p. 255). Humans are deeply invested in their worldviews existentially, and thus, this situation shapes how we interact with those deemed different from ourselves. Education can "invite a learner into understanding the self, the Other, and the relationship between the two" (Garrett, 2017, p. 3), and so it is important to engage with resistances to alternative viewpoints, including those that can arise from worldview threat in and out of the classroom.

Cultural worldviews are human-created, shared, symbolic conceptions of reality that infuse human existence with a sense of meaning and enduring significance. Aspects of worldviews can be religious or secular (e.g., creationism and intelligent design versus evolution), shared by a larger group (e.g., "Western society" or a national group like "Canadians") or limited to a niche culture (e.g., "goths" or "jocks"). The unique nexus of one's worldviews helps one cope with existential fear, and thus, humans can cling to their worldview(s) in ways that affect numerous social relations, such as "prejudice, nationalism, social judgments, interpersonal attraction, romantic love, charitable giving, emotional reactions to one's own creative actions, support for pre-emptive wars and suicide bombing (within different cultures of course), stereotyping... attributional biases, and other forms of behavior" (Pyszczynski,

Greenberg, Solomon, & Maxfield, 2006, p. 329; see also Greenberg, Solomon, & Arndt, 2007).

Worldviews prescribe standards and values that define what it means to be a respected member of the culture or group. By living up to these cultural values, people earn a sense of self-esteem, thus, self-esteem is the perception that one is a valued and protected member of the cultural meaning system. In other words, it is not personal, but rather social and relational. Becker (1975) argued that human beings have become symbolically re-instinctivized; humans socialize themselves into groups via a cultural meaning system. Thus, "unlike zebras and apes, people are not instinctually driven to belong to just any group of conspecifics; they want to be included in groups of like-minded individuals that provide much needed validation and support for their death-denying illusions" (Schimel & Greenberg, 2013, p. 289). This need to group ourselves due to diverging worldviews has caused great evils in the world.

Worldview Threat

The problem with adhering to cultural worldviews as an antidote for terror is that all worldviews are to some extent arbitrary, fictional, assemblages about the nature of reality, and thus require continual validation from others in order remain believable. To have an effective buffer against existential fear, one must believe in their worldview and its associated values, and then also believe that they are "meeting or exceeding the standards and values" (Burke et al., 2010, p. 155; see also Rosenblatt et al., 1989). Exposure to cultures of people with alternate worldviews, especially those that are diametrically opposed to one's own, therefore, potentially destabilizes one's faith in the dominant worldview and the psychological protection it provides. Contact with others who define reality in different ways undermines an assumed consensus for people's death-denying ideologies, and therefore (directly and/or indirectly) calls both one's worldview and source of self-esteem into question. It should be noted that worldview threat does not preclude other reasons for defensiveness, nor does it discount other uses of a worldview: TMT explains that "threats to meaning, certainty, belongingness, self-esteem, and other psychological entities produce fluid compensation effects because they are linked to the problem of death" (Pyszczynski, Greenberg, et al., 2006, p. 332). The key word here is "linked"—TMT does not rule out additional processes in play.

Because exposure to people with different worldviews can arouse a feeling of existential threat, there arises a need for defence (Solomon et al., 2015). Defensive reactions to a different worldview can vary, but TMT suggests at least four different types. The first is *assimilation*, which involves attempts to convert worldview-opposing others to our own system of belief. The prototypical example of assimilation is missionary work, and in education, this process can take the form of teachers (or fellow students) attempting to convert students to their perspective on historical or contemporary events, which is related to the idea of teaching as an immortality project (van Kessel & Burke, 2018). The second and most common method is *derogation*, which includes belittling individuals who espouse a different worldview. If we dismiss opposing views, we can dismiss their alternate views of reality as a threat to the validity of our own, and so in classrooms different cultural perspectives can be mocked or insulted. Historically, assimilation and derogation have often not been enough, especially considering that other groups are often just as unimpressed with our values and ideals as we are with theirs, further implying that our own way of life may not be the one, true way. Thus, a third more extreme method is *annihilation*, which entails aggressive action aimed at killing or injuring members of the threatening worldview (e.g., see Hayes, Schimel, & Williams, 2008; Pyszczynski, Abdollahi et al., 2006). If groups of people with opposing beliefs can be injured or killed, the implication is that their beliefs are truly inferior to our own. Further to this point, by eliminating large numbers of people with a different version of reality, the threatening worldview may cease to exist, and thus no longer pose a threat. Some of the most horrific human behaviours throughout history, namely war and genocide, are examples of annihilation as a form of worldview defence, and, in the classroom, students may express support for annihilation of certain groups. One final strategy of worldview defence that is less destructive than the previous three is termed *accommodation*, which is to modify one's own worldview to incorporate some aspects of the threatening worldview. More specifically, through accommodation one accepts some of the peripheral components of the threatening worldview into one's own, which renders the alternate worldview less threatening and at the same time allows one's core beliefs to remain intact. For example, upon repeated exposure to scientific evidence for evolution (vs. divine creation) as the origin of human life, a religious person might come to believe that evolution is correct, but that a divine creator had a hand in the process (e.g., the debate between macro- vs. micro-evolution). In this way, for example, those with religious beliefs can accept the correctness of a secular-scientific worldview without abandoning their core principles (see Hayes et al., 2015).

Defensive Reactions and Mortality Salience

Drawing from the MS hypothesis, reminders of death increase prejudice towards those deemed to be "others." As an example, Greenberg et al. (1990) found that reminding Christian participants of their own death increased their liking of a fellow Christian, but decreased their liking of a Jewish student. An additional study conceptually replicated this effect with a nationalistic worldview: U.S. participants who were reminded of their own death reported liking an interviewee who spoke positively about the U.S. political system more and reported liking an interviewee who spoke negatively about the U.S. political system less. These results also generalize to racial prejudice (Greenberg, Schimel, Martens, Solomon, & Pyszczynski, 2001).

Reminders of death might not only increase negative attitudes, but also actual aggression against worldview violators. MS can lead to the acceptance and support for violent intergroup conflict, even if it ends with mass civilian casualties. Indeed, humankind's "most tragic flaw" is "the inability to get along peacefully with those different from ourselves" (Greenberg et al., 2007, p. 117). In one set of studies investigating this possibility, McGregor and colleagues (1998) found that MS led participants to assign more hot sauce for another person to consume if they thought the person had an opposing (vs. supporting) political worldview. Even more disturbing are recent studies assessing whether MS would increase support for large-scale aggression against groups that are currently in conflict across the globe. Pyszczynski, Abdollahi, et al. (2006) found that MS increased Iranian participants' support for violence against U.S. citizens through a more positive evaluation of a pro-martyrdom student and increased willingness to consider joining the pro-martyrdom student's cause. In a subsequent study, researchers found a parallel effect among U.S. participants, with MS subjects increasing their support for extreme military actions (e.g., use of nuclear weaponry and pre-emptive strikes) against worldview threatening nations (e.g., Iran, North Korea, and Syria). U.S. participants reminded of their own impending death also said they were willing to sacrifice thousands of

138   C. van KESSEL

civilian lives if it led to the capture or killing of Osama bin Laden. Along similar lines, Hirschberger et al. (2016) found that when reminded of death, Israeli Jewish and South Korean participants were more supportive of retributive violence against Hamas and North Korea, respectively, when such acts were justified.

Discounting Other Views in a Classroom

Worldview challenges can be constants in classrooms due to the diversity of the humans in that environment. Furthermore, certain topics may highlight those differences (e.g., evolution vs. creationism in biology, contested or controversial issues in social studies), and classes might explore worldviews from different times, places, and contexts (e.g., in literature and history). Given that even the mention of a variety of worldviews can trigger existential threat, let alone the presentation of those different worldviews as viable alternative frameworks, the application of Becker's ideas and TMT directly in a classroom setting provides helpful opportunities. We can engage with multiple perspectives while recognizing, and possibly compensating for, defensive reactions that are not conducive to tolerance, respect, or nurturance of difference. In this way, knowledge of worldview threat might help us metacognitively anticipate our threat-and-defence cycle, and thus act more thoughtfully. Our fear of death is one specific source from where unhelpful reactions might arise, and thus presents an avenue for all to consider the ways in which humans, regardless of their identifications, might engage and learn from troubling initial reactions to perspectives and worldviews different than their own.

Our worldview protects us from the fear of death, and therefore leads to a tendency to discount, or even attack, other worldviews (and their proponents) that challenge our own. TMT posits that even the mere existence of different worldviews, let alone a direct engagement with them, can interfere with the anxiety-buffering function of the cultural worldview (Greenberg, Simon, Pyszczynski, Solomon, & Chatel, 1992). In other words, banal encounters with a different worldview can trigger defensive reactions like derogation. This situation appears bleak, but there is converging evidence that anxiety-induced intolerance can be countered by fostering and rewarding tolerance as an aspect of the cultural worldview by making tolerance both a value and a highly accessible option (Greenberg et al., 1992, p. 218). Although teachers cannot (and should not be expected to) create worldviews for their students, they can create a classroom environment that has the potential to tap into existing worldviews that move beyond tolerance to a state of learning from difference.

Two Concluding Quotations

Although all hope for humanity cannot rest on education (or worse still, one specific teacher-saviour), there are opportunities to engage with theories and practices that facilitate peaceful and productive relations with groups different from ourselves. As James Baldwin (1962) eloquently wrote:

> Perhaps the whole root of our trouble, the human trouble, is that we will sacrifice all the beauty of our lives, will imprison ourselves in totems, taboos, crosses, blood sacrifices, steeples, mosques, races, armies, flags, nations, in order to deny the fact of death, which is the only fact we have. It seems to me that one ought to rejoice in the *fact* of death—ought to decide, indeed, to *earn* one's death by confronting with passion the conundrum of life. (para. 50)

Ernest Becker and TMT can help us accept that fate, and thus also can help us live on this planet with more grace in our human relations and perhaps beyond. As humans, we seek immortality—literal and symbolic—and those can have disastrous consequences. Baldwin (1962) noted that we "imprison" ourselves in aspects of nationalism and our worldviews. Yet, such a situation does not need to be the case. By reframing our lives as earning death, instead of running from it, we might feel freer to live together in ways that hurt less. Part of this process would be to embrace our creatureliness, following Simon Critchley's (2009) advice:

> We cannot return the unasked-for gifts of nature and culture. Nor can we jump over the shadow of our mortality. But we can transform the manner in which we accept those gifts and we can stand more fully in the light that casts that shadow. It is my wager that if we can begin to accept our limitedness, then we might be able to give up certain of the fantasies of infantile omnipotence, worldly wealth and puffed-up power that culminate in both aggressive personal conflicts and bloody wars between opposed and exclusive gods. To be a creature is to accept our dependence and

140   C. van KESSEL

limitedness in a way that does not result in disaffection and despair. It is rather the condition for courage and endurance. (pp. 248–249)

Although we cannot change the world as it is right now or the fact that we will die someday, like Baldwin's (1962) call to free ourselves from our destructive societal constraints, Critchley (2009) provokes us to embrace our status as limited creatures. Instead of harming ourselves, each other, and the planet in the vain attempt to deny our death, we might rather pluck up the courage to accept our eventual doom. Abandoning futile and destructive immortality projects can alleviate some of the conditions that plague human societies as well as our individual relations with others. By whatever mechanism one might believe in, humans possess the double-edged sword of the knowledge of our mortality. Even in attempting to escape it, death "is with us *because* we are trying to escape it" (May, 2009, p. 7). That fact will not change. What can change is our acceptance of that knowledge—that we are animals whose ultimate fate is determined—and that we can make our classrooms (and societies) hurt less.

REFERENCES

Bailey, M. (1946). The teacher's immortality. *Education, 66*(8), 115.

Baldwin, J. (1962, November 17). Letter from a region in my mind. *The New Yorker*. Retrieve from http://www.newyorker.com/magazine/1962/11/17/letter-from-a-region-in-my-mind.

Becker, E. (1973). *The denial of death*. New York, NY: Free Press.

Becker, E. (1975). *Escape from evil*. New York, NY: Free Press.

Biesta, G. (2010). *Good education in an age of measurement: Ethics, politics, democracy*. Boulder, CO: Paradigm.

Blacker, D. J. (1997). *Dying to teach: The educator's search for immortality*. New York, NY: Teachers College.

Bregman, L. (1985). Academic 'immortality' and the eschatological destiny of the dead. *Religion and Intellectual Life, 2*(3), 28–36.

Britzman, D. P. (1986). Cultural myths in the making of a teacher: Biography and social structure in teacher education. *Harvard Educational Review, 56*, 442–456.

Burke, B. L., Martens, A., & Faucher, E. H. (2010). Two decade of terror management theory: A meta-analysis of mortality salience research. *Personality and Social Psychology Review, 14*, 155–195. https://doi.org/10.1177/1088868309352321.

7 EVIL, EXISTENTIAL TERROR, AND CLASSROOM CLIMATE 141

Burke, K. J., & Segall, A. (2015). Teaching as Jesus making: The hidden curriculum of Christ in schooling. *Teachers College Record, 117*(3), 1–27.

Butterfield, E. W. (1921). The teacher's immortality. *The Journal of Education, 94*(11), 289–290. https://doi.org/10.1177/002205742109401105.

Ciaccio, J. (2000). A teacher's chance for immortality. *Education Digest, 65*(6), 44.

Clandinin, D. J., & Connelly, F. M. (1996). Teachers' professional knowledge landscapes: Teacher stories—Stories of teachers—School stories—Stories of schools. *Educational Researcher, 25*(3), 24–30.

Critchley, S. (2009). *The book of dead philosophers.* New York, NY: Vintage.

Dahlbeck, J. (2015). Educating for immortality: Spinoza and the pedagogy of gradual existence. *Journal of Philosophy of Education, 49*(3), 347–365. https://doi.org/10.1111/1467-9752.12107.

Donald, D. T. (2009). The curricular problem of Indigenousness: Colonial frontier logics, teacher resistances, and the acknowledgement of ethical space. In J. Nahachewsky & I. Johnston (Eds.), *Beyond "presentism": Re-imagining the historical, personal, and social places of curriculum* (pp. 23–41). Rotterdam, The Netherlands: Sense.

Farber, B. (1991). *Crisis in education.* San Francisco, CA: Jossey-Bass.

Freire, P. (1989). *Pedagogy of the oppressed.* New York, NY: Continuum.

Fritsche, J., Jonas, E., Fisher, P., Koranyi, N., Berger, N., & Fleischmann, B. (2007). Mortality salience and the desire for offspring. *Journal of Experimental Social Psychology, 43*(5), 753–762. https://doi.org/10.1016/j.jesp.2006.10.003.

Fullan, M. G. (1993). Why teachers must become change agents. *Educational Leadership, 50*(6), 1–13.

Garrett, H. J. (2017). *Learning to be in the world with others: Difficult knowledge and social studies education.* New York, NY: Peter Lang.

Greenberg, J., Pyszczynski, T., & Solomon, S. (1986). The causes and consequences of a need for self-esteem: A terror management theory. In R. F. Baumeister (Ed.), *Public self and private self* (pp. 189–212). New York, NY: Springer.

Greenberg, J., Pyszczynski, T., Solomon, S., Rosenblatt, A., Veeder, M., Kirkland, S., & Lyon, D. (1990). Evidence for terror management theory II: The effects of mortality salience on reaction to those who threaten or bolster the cultural worldview. *Journal of Personality and Social Psychology, 58*, 308–318. https://doi.org/10.1037/0022-3514.58.2.308.

Greenberg, J., Schimel, J., Martens, A., Solomon, S., & Pyszczynski, T. (2001). Sympathy for the devil: Evidence that reminding whites of their mortality projects promotes more favorable reactions to white racists. *Motivation and Emotion, 25*(2), 113–133. https://doi.org/10.1023/A:1010613909207.

Greenberg, J., Simon, L., Pyszczynski, T., Solomon, S., & Chatel, D. (1992). Terror management theory and tolerance: Does mortality salience always intensify negative reactions to others who threaten one's worldview? *Journal of Personality and Social Psychology, 63*, 212–220. https://doi.org/10.1037/0022-3514.63.2.212.

142   C. VAN KESSEL

Greenberg, J., Solomon, S., & Arndt, J. (2007). A uniquely human motivation: Terror management. In J. Shah & W. Gardner (Eds.), *Handbook of motivation science* (pp. 114–134). New York, NY: Guilford.

Hayes, J., Schimel, J., & Williams, T. (2008). Fighting death with death: The buffering effects of learning that worldview violators have died. *Psychological Science, 19*(5), 501–507. https://doi.org/10.1111/j.1467-9280.2008.02115.x.

Hayes, J., Schimel, J., Williams, T., Howard, A. L., Webber, D., & Faucher, E. H. (2015). Worldview accommodation: Selectively modifying committed beliefs provides defense against worldview threat. *Self and Identity, 14*(5), 521–548. https://doi.org/10.1080/15298868.2015.1036919.

Heflick, N. A., Goldenberg, J. L., Cooper, D. P., & Puvia, E. (2011). From women to objects: Appearance focus, target gender, and perceptions of warmth, morality and competence. *Journal of Experimental Social Psychology, 47*(3), 572–581. https://doi.org/10.1016/j.jesp.2010.12.020.

Hirschberger, G., Pyszczynski, T., Ein-Dor, T., Shani Sherman, T., Kadah, E., Kesebir, P., & Park, Y. C. (2016). Fear of death amplifies retributive justice motivations and encourages political violence. *Peace and Conflict: Journal of Peace Psychology, 22*, 67–74. https://doi.org/10.1037/pac0000129.

Howard, S., & Johnson, B. (2004). Resilient teachers: Resisting stress and burnout. *Social Psychology of Education, 7*, 399–420. https://doi.org/10.1007/s11218-004-0975-0.

Liechty, D. (2015). Biography. *Ernest Becker Foundation.* Retrieved from http://ernestbecker.org/about-becker/biography/.

Madden, B. (2016). *(Un)becoming teacher of school-based Aboriginal education: Early career teachers, teacher identify, and Aboriginal education across institutions* (Unpublished doctoral dissertation). University of British Columbia, Vancouver, Canada.

May, T. (2009). *Death.* New York, NY: Routledge.

McGregor, H., Lieberman, J. D., Solomon, S., Greenberg, J., Arndt, J., Simon, L., & Pyszczynski, T. (1998). Terror management and aggression: Evidence that mortality salience motivates aggression against worldview threatening others. *Journal of Personality and Social Psychology, 74*, 590–605. https://doi.org/10.1037/0022-3514.74.3.590.

Plutarch. (1927). *De auditu* (F. C. Babbitt, Trans). Cambridge, MA: Harvard University Press (Loeb Classical Library). Retrieved from http://penelope.uchicago.edu/Thayer/E/Roman/Texts/Plutarch/Moralia/De_auditu*.html.

Pyszczynski, T., Abdollahi, A., Solomon, S., Greenberg, J., Cohen, F., & Weise, D. (2006). Mortality salience, martyrdom, and military might: The great Satan versus the axis of evil. *Personality and Social Psychology Bulletin, 32*, 525–537. https://doi.org/10.1177/0146167205282157.

Pyszczynski, T., Greenberg, J., & Solomon, S. (1999). A dualprocess model of defense against conscious and unconscious death-related thoughts: An extension of terror management theory. *Psychological Review, 106*, 835–845.

Pyszczynski, T., Greenberg, J., Solomon, S., & Maxfield, M. (2006). On the unique psychological import of the human awareness of mortality: Theme and variations. *Psychological Inquiry, 17*, 328–356. https://doi.org/10.1080/10478400701369542.

Roberts, P. (2008). Life, death, and transformation: Education and incompleteness in Herman Hesse's 'The Glass Bead Game'. *Canadian Journal of Education, 31*(3), 667–696.

Roberts, T.-A., Goldenberg, J. L., Power, C., & Pyszczynski, T. (2002). "Feminine protection": The effects of menstruation on attitudes toward women. *Psychology of Women Quarterly, 26*(2), 131–139. https://doi.org/10.1111/1471-6402.00051\.

Rosenblatt, A., Greenberg, J., Solomon, S., Pyszczynski, T., & Lyon, D. (1989). Evidence for terror management theory: I. The effects of mortality salience on reactions to those who violate or uphold cultural values. *Journal of Personality and Social Psychology, 57*, 681–690. https://doi.org/10.1037/0022-3514.57.4.681.

Schimel, J., & Greenberg, J. (2013). The birth and death of belonging. In C. N. DeWall (Ed.), *The Oxford handbook of social exclusion.* New York, NY: Oxford. https://doi.org/10.1093/oxfordhb/9780195398700.013.0027.

Schimel, J., Hayes, J., & Sharp, M. (2018). A consideration of three critical hypotheses. In C. Routledge & M. Vess (Eds.), *The handbook of terror management theory* (pp. 1–25). London, UK: Academic Press.

Schimel, J., Hayes, J., Williams, T., & Jahrig, J. (2007). Is death really the worm at the core? Converging evidence that worldview threat increases death-thought accessibility. *Journal of Personality and Social Psychology, 92*(5), 789–803. https://doi.org/10.1037/0022-3514.92.5.789.

Solomon, S., Greenberg, J., & Pyszczynski, T. (2015). *The worm at the core: On the role of death in life.* New York, NY: Random House.

van Kessel, C., & Burke, K. (2018). Teaching as immortality project: Positing weakness in response to terror. *Journal of Philosophy of Education, 52*(2), 216–229. https://doi.org/10.1111/1467-9752.12301.

Webber, D., Zhang, R., Schimel, J., & Blatter, J. (2016). Finding death in meaninglessness: Evidence that death-thought accessibility increases in response to meaning threats. *British Journal of Social Psychology, 55*(1), 144–161. https://doi.org/10.1111/bjso.12118.

CHAPTER 8

Epilogue

In this book, I have asked readers to consider how different understandings of evil might shape how we live together, which I see as a fundamental line of inquiry in education. In his book, *Learning to Be in the World with Others*, H. James Garrett (2017) asked us: "How do we come to understand the complicated world in which we live? What do ideas do to us and what does that doing mean for what we think of as our responsibility to and with others?" (p. 133). The study of evil—how we might understand it as a process, and how exploring this topic can affect us—is one piece of the puzzle whereby we explore the sort of relations we want to have with others. When evil is a process within the domain of human activity, there is an opportunity to examine the roots and manifestations of evil in a way that encourages us to actively do something about it. When evil is confined to the supernatural or to extraordinary humans beyond what we can relate to, it can be disempowering. Although an uncomfortable thought, knowing that evil can be ordinary and perpetuated by individuals like us (and groups like the ones we are part of) can frame discussions in a way that illuminates our own responsibility to take care of others.

Evil as a word and a concept has tremendous power. The word evokes cognitive effects as well as emotional and bodily affects, and, therefore, needs to be used with caution. The politics of evil (see Chapter 5) reveals how those in power might abuse the label of evil for their own ends (e.g., Bernstein, 2005). Some have argued that we ought to avoid the

© The Author(s) 2019

C. van Kessel, *An Education in 'Evil'*,

Palgrave Studies in Educational Futures,

https://doi.org/10.1007/978-3-030-16605-2_8

word altogether (e.g., Shaw, 2019), and understandably so. Without a way to think through evil, that word can shut down our critical thinking about the complexities of our human situation and social interactions: *Why did that horrible thing happen? Because that person/group was evil. End of story.* Others may also call for societies to abandon the idea of evil but for a different reason: evil as too subjective. Friedrich Nietzsche (1886/2006, 1887/2006), is perhaps the most (in)famous in this latter camp of thinking. He believed that the concepts of both good and evil stifle creativity and accomplishment, and that the concept of evil is merely a product of negative emotions (*ressentiment*—a combination of envy, hatred, and resentment), and the labelling as such is for revenge more so than something more productive. This view is not without merit. In fact, my appreciation for Baudrillard's work (see Chapter 6) stems from a similar critique, but Baudrillard separates moral evil from *Symbolic Evil*, the former of which is less helpful than the latter.

Regardless of the critiques against engaging with the idea of evil, my feeling (obviously) is that it is still worthy of study, so long as we avoid simply dictating or parroting simplistic moral standards. If we take the time to ascertain how conceptualizations of evil can be helpful in particular instances (rather than being fixated on precisely defining *this* or *that* as evil), then we have an opportunity to sit in the tension of actions (or inactions) that we find repulsive and/or troubling. We cannot discard the term, for example, simply because of misuse. Claudia Card (2010) aptly noted that: "If the likelihood of the ideological abuse of a concept were sufficient reason to abandon the concept, we should probably abandon all normative concepts, certainly 'right' and 'wrong'" (p. 15). Rather than thinking or feeling less about evil, let us sit with our uncomfortable effects and affects and then, perhaps, be more inclined to change our circumstances so that such evils cannot occur in the first place.

By studying evil, we keep the possibilities for goodness open to a variety of interpretations. A focus on how to live a good life can be prescriptive (although not necessarily so). When living well is framed as how to we *should* live, or even more so, how we should live our *best* lives, then the task seems prescribed, likely by normative measures. In that way, we can foreclose possibilities for other ways of being in the world. So, here lies the advantage of the opposite approach. Examining that which we want to avoid provides some structure as to how we might live as individuals and as folks together in societies, and yet it does not offer a definitive answer. Instead, we are invited to respond in countless ways, and yet

8 EPILOGUE   147

with the shared commitment to treat each other in respectful and helpful manners. Education has a role to play as we muddle our way through the "perpetual challenges and hopes" of finding ways to respect and understand other humans as well as other entities with whom we share this planet (Hodgson, Vlieghe, & Zamojski, 2017, p. 16). Studying evil is not perfect, however. In some ways, a focus on evil could yoke our discussions to the status quo—many humans have been, and continue to be, very hurtful to others—and yet I hope that seeing evil as a *process* undergone by people much like ourselves (more so than a *thing*) affords us the interrelated possibilities of withholding externalizing judgement and thus (re)considering the roles we might play in our own lives as well as committing to "a renewal of our common world" (Hodgson et al., 2017, p. 18). The conversation becomes as much about us ourselves as it does whatever instance of evil we might be examining.

Perhaps for some it is tempting to seek a singular definition of evil. Certainly, it can be for me at times, especially when the instance of evil strikes a chord in my own heart. It is difficult to know when emotional responses are helping or harming (at least for me). It also occurs to me that many seek the comfort of a single answer over and above a multitude of possible responses. Again, I claim no superiority here, simply that I assume that because I have struggled with this issue, then others must as well. From the process of conducting the research contained in this book, I have grown to appreciate complex non-answers as much as something explicitly tangible to grasp. I am not, however, without my opinions of which conceptualizations of evil are more helpful than others, and yet I hesitate to discount particular conceptualizations because the problem itself is so complex. For me, the issue is how an understanding of evil can help us thwart it—not finding a way to categorize for the sake of categorizing.

Each chapter in this book considered particular understandings of evil and how these conceptualizations might affect us. These discussions have centred around how all of us are capable of: thoughtlessly perpetuating suffering (Arendt, 1963/2006), harming others intentionally when triggered by our existential fears (Becker, 1975), failing to uphold our truth procedures or forcing our truths upon others (Badiou, 1993/2001), or flattening the creative potential of *Symbolic Evil* (Baudrillard, 1990/1993, 2004/2005). From my study of how some high school students conceptualize evil, it is clear that there are many understandings floating around about what evil can and might be, and that conversations

148   C. van KESSEL

about evil provide an important opportunity for educators to arrange curriculum in ways that open up the possibilities for students to expand beyond what we claim to teach them. Engaging with ethical questions that arise from the study of evil at the personal and societal level encourages us:

> to explicitly question the diverse and multiple relationships of selves and the social.... [and thus] participate more knowingly in questions of social life with an interpretation of the ways we all are implicated in the material conditions that shape what and how we claim to know. (den Heyer, 2009, p. 34)

There is much that students (and indeed us all) already know about evil, and yet we are rarely invited to contemplate how our ideas about evil affect us and our presence in the world. If, as the popular saying (misattributed to W. B. Yeats, but valuable nonetheless) states, "Education is not the filling of a pail, but the lighting of a fire," then evil is very provocative material for kindling.

References

Arendt, H. (2006). *Eichmann in Jerusalem: A report on the banality of evil.* New York, NY: Penguin. (Original work published in 1963)

Badiou, A. (2001). *Ethics: An essay on the understanding of evil* (P. Hallward, Trans.). London, UK: Verso. (Original work published in 1993)

Baudrillard, J. (1993). *The transparency of evil* (J. Benedict, Trans.). London, UK: Verso. (Original work published in 1990)

Baudrillard, J. (2005). *The intelligence of evil or the lucidity pact* (C. Turner, Trans.). Oxford, UK: Berg. (Original work published in 2004)

Becker, E. (1975). *Escape from evil.* New York, NY: Free Press.

Bernstein, R. J. (2005). *The abuse of evil: The corruption of politics and religion since 9/11.* Malden, MA: Polity.

Card, C. (2010). *Confronting evils: Terrorism, torture, genocide.* Cambridge, UK: Cambridge University Press.

den Heyer, K. (2009). Implicated and called upon: Challenging an educated position of self, others, knowledge and knowing as things to acquire. *Critical Literacy: Theories and Practices, 3*(1), 26–35.

Garrett, H. J. (2017). *Learning to be in the world with others: Difficult knowledge and social studies education.* New York, NY: Peter Lang.

Hodgson, N., Vlieghe, J., & Zamojski, P. (2017). *Manifesto for the post-critical pedagogy.* London: punctum.

Nietzsche, F. (2006). Beyond good and evil: Prelude to a philosophy of the future. In K. A. Pearson & D. Large (Eds.), *The Nietzsche reader* (pp. 311–359). Malden, MA: Blackwell. (Original work published in 1886)

Nietzsche, F. (2006). On the genealogy of morality: A polemic. In K. A. Pearson & D. Large (Eds.), *The Nietzsche reader* (pp. 390–435). Malden, MA: Blackwell. (Original work published in 1887)

Shaw, J. (2019, February 15). Evil is in the eye of the beholder. *The Globe and Mail*. Retrieved from https://www.theglobeandmail.com/opinion/article-evil-is-in-the-eye-of-the-beholder.

INDEX

A
Abnormal evil, 89, 96–99, 102
Action (in Arendt's sense), 39, 46, 51, 57, 74
Advanced Placement European History, 53–54
Agency, 3, 10, 26, 45–46, 48–53, 68, 75, 78, 98, 99, 115
Anti-Semitism, 53
Arendt, Hannah, 8, 12, 37–42, 48–46, 51–53, 55–57, 65, 74, 97, 147
Aristotle, 45
Axis of Evil, 83, 99, 100

B
Badiou, Alain, 3, 13, 23, 63–79, 147
Baldwin, James, 139–140
Banality of evil, 8, 12, 37–48, 51, 55, 57, 74, 97. *See also* Arendt, Hannah
Baudrillard, Jean, 13, 107–121, 146, 147

Becker, Ernest, 13, 125–128, 132, 134–135, 138–139, 147
Bernstein, Richard, 4, 21–22, 38–39, 145
Betrayal, Badiou's understanding of, 13, 63, 71, 73
Biesta, Gert, 3, 50, 77, 118, 132. *See also* Subjectification
Black Panther (motion picture), 26, 28–29
Black Panther Party, 114
Britzman, Deborah P., 2, 56, 86, 96–97, 133
Browning, Christopher, 42, 47
Bush, George W. *See* Axis of Evil
Butler, Judith, 2

C
Card, Claudia, 20, 146
Citizenship education, 13, 50, 63–65, 74, 76–79

© The Editor(s) (if applicable) and The Author(s), 151
under exclusive license to Springer Nature Switzerland AG 2019
C. van Kessel, *An Education in 'Evil'*,
Palgrave Studies in Educational Futures,
https://doi.org/10.1007/978-3-030-16605-2

152 INDEX

Classroom applications
of Arendt and villainification, 46–55
of Baudrillard's *Symbolic Evil*, 114–115, 118–121
of worldview threat and defence, 135–138
Coalition of the Youth of the Revolution, 115
Columbus, Christopher, 50–51
as related to Forbes' discussion of *Wétiko*, 24–25
Critchley, Simon, 69, 139–140
Critical pedagogy. *See* Critical theory
Critical theory, 64–65, 79, 120–121
Critical thinking, 3, 4, 10, 39, 45, 50, 54, 99–100, 102, 114, 120–121, 146
Critical thought(fulness). *See* Critical thinking

D

Dark Knight, The (motion picture), 27–28
Darth Vader, 26, 87, 95
Deleuze, Gilles, & Guattari, Félix, 13, 83–84, 101
Demonizing, 29, 51
Demons/demonic (or not being), 40, 42, 87
den Heyer, Kent, 50, 68, 69, 74–76, 78, 148
Difficult knowledge, 1, 12, 56, 86. *See also* Britzman, Deborah, P.
Discomfort, 2, 29, 44, 45, 57, 97, 129, 134, 146
Disempowerment, 31, 98, 115, 145
Dracula, 31–32

E

Eichmann, Adolf, 37, 41–42, 45–46, 87, 97
Emotions, 1, 3, 7, 8, 22, 44, 56, 92, 100, 134, 145. *See also* Feelings
Ethics, 1, 7–9, 11, 20, 23, 24, 33, 45–46, 50–52, 54, 63, 66–68, 70, 76, 148
Etymology of evil, 2
Evil Empire. *See* Reagan, Ronald
Existential fear. *See* Fear, of death

F

Farley, Lisa, 2, 3, 8
Fear, 5, 45, 54, 56, 90, 100, 102, 103, 112, 116
of death, 13, 126–131, 134, 135, 138, 147
Feelings, 22, 136, 146
of agency, 3, 44, 98, 99. *See also* agency
of guilt, 7, 56
linked to evil, 91, 99, 100, 146
of significance in the world, 131
See also Emotions
Fetishizing evil, 42

G

Garrett, H.J. (Jim), 134, 145
Genocide, 1, 7, 8, 20, 29, 42, 45, 46, 54, 66, 83, 96, 99, 113, 136. *See also* Holocaust
Guattari, Félix. *See* Deleuze, Gilles & Guattari, Félix

H

Heroification, 31, 43–45, 57
Historical thinking, 50

INDEX 153

Hitler, Adolf, 50, 53, 54, 85, 87, 93–97, 99
Holocaust, The, 5, 7, 9, 10, 20, 40–42, 47, 50, 54, 66, 98
Hyperindividualism. *See* Individual responsibility

I
Immortality, 128
  project, 131, 140
  teaching as, 125, 130–134, 136
Individual responsibility, 8, 25, 39, 43, 44, 46–50, 52, 54–57, 68, 71, 78, 96–98, 115, 133
Intent (to do evil), 3, 12, 19–21, 22–23, 25, 39, 42, 44–45, 48, 73, 93–96, 101, 103, 108, 109
Islamic State of Iraq and the Levant (ISIL), 57, 102

J
jagodzinski, jan, 26, 30
Joker, The, 27–28, 29

K
Kant, Immanuel, 11, 12, 19, 21–23, 25–26, 33, 38, 109
Killmonger, 26, 28–30

L
Lear, Jonathan. *See* Radical hope
Learning
  contemporary and historical events, 7, 38
  facts, 78, 97
  obedience and disobedience, 54–55
  potential for new, 74, 94, 102

Lisbon earthquake, 20. *See also* Natural disasters
Literacy (political), 10, 84, 99, 103, 118. *See also* Qualification

M
Mahfouz, Asmaa, 115
May, Todd, 33, 128, 131, 140
Media (power of). *See* Power of media
Minnich, Elizabeth, 13, 38, 42, 45
Monster (status as a), 20, 27, 32, 42, 48, 73
Moral
  education, 11, 99
  evil, 20, 107–110, 146
  failings, 2, 27, 31, 49, 50, 54
  law, 21–23, 38. *See also* Kant, Immanuel

N
Natural disasters, 20, 92, 93
Nazis, 6, 8, 11, 24, 37–42, 48, 52–55, 66, 72, 97, 99, 102, 125
Neiman, Susan, 19
Nietzsche, Friedrich, 146
Nosferatu, 31, 87

O
Order Police, The, 47
Order-words, 83–84, 101, 103
Ordinary evil. *See* Banality of evil

P
Perversion, 22, 110
  of the Good, 67, 73. *See also* Badiou, Alain
Phenomenography, 85–88

154 INDEX

Pinar, William (Bill), 65, 119
Plutarch, 132
Political rhetoric. *See* Rhetoric
of evil
Pol Pot, 50, 87, 93
Power
of media, 26
of the label evil, 3, 10–11, 13, 52–
54, 83–85, 89, 91, 102–103
of *Symbolic Evil*, 107, 109, 111
Precarity. *See* Butler, Judith
Privilege, 64, 68, 75, 78
Procrustes, 73

Q
Qualification, 76, 78, 118, 132. *See
also* Biesta, Gert
Questioning power, 3, 41, 54, 76,
111, 114, 120

R
Racism, 8, 25, 28, 44, 47–49, 53, 79,
99, 101, 137
Radical evil, 8, 20
Arendt's radical evil, 37, 38
Kant's radical evil, 11, 19, 21–23
Radical hope, 2
Reagan, Ronald, 83
Reality, 69, 85, 108, 112, 120,
134–136
Residential Schools, 43, 48–50, 73
Responsibility, 3, 7, 11, 38, 41,
43–45, 47, 51–52, 54–57, 65,
75–76, 78, 99
Rhetoric of evil, 56, 83, 84, 91, 92,
99, 101–103

S
Shattuck, Roger, 20–21
Shoah. *See* Holocaust, The

Simulacrum
Badiou's understanding of, 13, 74
Baudrillard's understanding of, 108
Slavery, 1, 7, 9, 20, 43, 77
Socialization, 11, 54, 65, 68, 76, 78,
118, 132, 135. *See also* Biesta,
Gert
Social studies curriculum and text-
books, 5–7, 49, 56, 64, 83–85,
99, 138
Standardized tests, 116, 119
Staub, Ervin, 20
Student
agency. *See* Agency
relation to historical figures, 31, 45,
98, 115
understandings of evil, 6, 46, 50, 92
Subjectification, 3, 75, 118, 133. *See
also* Biesta, Gert
Subjectivity, 51, 73, 88, 89
of evil, 5, 94–96, 103, 146

T
Teacher-as-saviour, 133, 134, 138, 139.
See also Immortality, teaching as
Terror
Badiou's understanding of, 13, 63,
71, 72
existential. *See* Fear, of death
Reign of, 114, 115
War on, 83, 112
Terrorism, 112
Terror management theory, 128–130,
139
Truth and Reconciliation Commission
of Canada (TRC), 49
Twilight (book series), 32

U
Uncertainty, 1, 109, 120, 129, 135,
139

INDEX 155

Uncomfortable. *See* Discomfort
Unknown (as an evil), 47, 89–91

V
Vampires, 31–32, 90, 93, 95
Villainification, 13, 38, 43–57, 97
Voldemort, 26, 87, 95

W
Wétiko, 12, 19, 24–25, 33
Wolverine, The, 30–31

Worldview, 5, 11, 92, 127–128
   threat and defence, 13, 43, 125,
    129–130, 134–139
Wynter, Sylvia, 51–52

X
X-Men (motion picture), 30–31

Y
Youth disengagement, 116–119
Youths, 26, 84, 89, 98, 99, 115